WRITE YOUR BOOK IN NO TIME

ALSO BY ANDRAE D. SMITH JR.

Facing Racism
The Guide to Overcoming Unconscious Bias & Hidden
Prejudice to Be a Part of the Change

The Entrepreneur's Guide to Finishing a
High-Impact Book While Running Your Business

Write Your Book in *No Time*

Andrae D. Smith Jr.

KB
Khrusos Books

Colorado Springs, CO, USA

Copyright © Andrae D. Smith, Jr., 2021

All rights reserved. No part of this publication may be reproduced or transmitted in any form or by any means, mechanical or electronic, including photocopying or recording, or by any information storage and retrieval system, or transmitted by email without permission in writing from the author.

Published 2021

ISBN: 978-0578989976 (Paperback)

DISCLAIMER

Neither the author nor the publisher assumes any responsibility for errors, omissions, or contrary interpretations of the subject matter herein. Any perceived slight of any individual or organization is purely unintentional. The events and conversations in this book have been set down from memory to the best of the author's ability, although some names and details have been changed to protect the privacy of individuals and referenced parties.

Brand and product names are trademarks or registered trademarks of their respective owners.

Cover Design: Emily's World of Design

Interior Author Headshot: Laura Lim Photography

To my Greatest-Grandma,
Lue W. Dobbins
(1926 – 2021)
I hope you're proud of this little nut.

"Decide what you want to do. Then decide to do it. Then do it."

—William Knowlton Zinsser,
On Writing Well: The Classic Guide to Writing Nonfiction

CONTENTS

Preface — xiii

1. YOUR TIME IS NOW — 1
2. THE BOOK LIFE CHOSE ME — 7
    Finding My Path — 7
    Becoming an Author — 10
3. THE ILLUMINATION METHOD — 15
    The Road Ahead — 19
    What This Book Is — 20
    What This Book Is Not — 21
4. WHY A BOOK? — 23
    Why Do We Read? — 23
    What Is a Book? — 26
    Why Are You Writing? — 29
    Activity — 32
5. CREATE SPACE — 35
    Busting the "No Time" Myth — 36
    If There's So Much Time, Why Don't I See It? — 37
    Bending Time — 45
    Activity — 51
6. IDENTIFY AND DEFINE YOUR READER — 53
    Understand the Ideal Reader — 56
    Identify and Define Your IR — 59
    Activity — 67
7. CHOOSE YOUR BOOK'S TOPIC — 69
    Activity — 76
8. STRUCTURE AND CONTENT — 77
    The Shape of a Book — 78
    The Intro and Conclusion — 82

The Core Content	88
Activity	93
9. READY TO WRITE	97
Find Your Flow	98
How You Write	101
Your Unique Success Plan	103
Activity	106
10. WRITING YOUR FIRST DRAFT	109
Tell Stories	111
Connect the Dots	116
Build Chapters Before You Write	118
Use Your Own Voice	121
Be Open to Inspiration	123
ACTIVITY	124
11. EDITING SECRETS	127
Developmental Editing	128
Line Editing	129
Copyediting	130
Proofreading	131
12. TITLE, DESCRIPTION, AND COVER DESIGN	135
Naming Your Book	136
Describing Your Book	139
Create Your Short Bio	142
Cover Art	145
Activity	148
13. WRITER'S BLOCK OR WRITING BLOCKS?	149
I. Getting Stuck at the Intro or Conclusion	153
II. Can't Think of Good Stories	154
III. Getting Stuck in an Editing Cycle	154
IV. Allowing Distractions	156
V. Not Running the Plan	156
VI. Imposter Syndrome	157
14. CONCLUSION	161

Acknowledgments	169
Thank You	171
About the Author	175
Appendix 1	179
Appendix 2	183
Notes	187

PREFACE

> *Anything can be possible with the right attitude, the right strategy, and the right implementation. If you're struggling to reach your goals, the issue is almost always one of those."*

It was nearing the end of July 2021, and I was just wrapping up a two-week launch for my new book-writing beta program. In this beta, I was looking for three or four coaches, healers, or movement leaders who wanted to write and publish their nonfiction books in the next ninety days. This was *two months* shorter than my flagship program, and many people were intrigued by this offer—or more specifically, by the promise.

During the campaign, I must have had a dozen or so conversations with people who seemed genuinely interested in how they could finish a book so quickly. Books take months, sometimes years, to create, and I was telling them that they could finish one, A-to-Z, in a fraction of that time. There had to be some catch. There was just no way.

"So what's your secret, Andrae?" one of these aspiring

authors asked me during a video call. "How do you know it's possible?"

"Oh, that's easy." I smiled and went into my spiel. "I've done it. I wrote my first book, *Facing Racism*, in just seven days and published it just three months later. I became a bestseller in just a few hours." I had said these lines so many times, I practically knew them by heart.

He looked at me in a way that, even through the webcam, suggested his curiosity and betrayed his distrust. "Wow. You must be a robot, man. I don't think I could write that fast."

"No, it's not necessarily about writing speed. It's about having the right plan. Most new authors struggle to write their books because they have no idea what they're doing or what they want to say. They have all of these ideas in their heads because they know their material. They're subject matter experts, but book-writing is new territory. Nine times out of ten, I'm certain the ones who don't finish or who take years to get done don't have a good plan to get them past the first draft. If you get there, the rest is easy."

"So how do I get there?" he asked, sitting forward a little.

He was really listening. *I might actually get him into the program*, I thought. I shared my screen and walked him through my framework, showing him how surprisingly simple it is. I told him it's almost elementary, and the only reason he, or anyone, couldn't do it, is that they just haven't been taught how to apply this method for books. When I finished the walk-through, he put his hand to his chin, thinking.

"It makes perfect sense when you explain it."

Of course it does, I thought.

"So… How much time does all this take? My biggest challenge is that there's no real room in my schedule. I'm running my business most of the day, and when I'm not, I'm not really trying to think about work. You can help me get all of this done?"

"Yep! It only takes a few focused hours each week, and I'll be with you the entire way to make sure you maximize the little time you have."

"Okay… This looks great… I'll have to think about it, though. I'm just not sure I can fit a book into my schedule right now."

At this point I could have asked to see his schedule and tried to break down his limiting beliefs. I knew we could get his book done, but something told me that he wasn't going to sign up that day, so I gently guided the conversation to a close.

At first, I was a little bummed that he hadn't joined the program; he would have written a really great book. Had I not been clear enough? Did I miss something that would have made it a no-brainer for him? Maybe I explained too much? After watching the call recording, I reasoned that even if he had joined, he wouldn't have gotten the maximum benefits of the program. We had the right strategy, but his mindset wasn't there yet. He wasn't convinced that *he* could succeed.

Our conversation got me thinking… He wasn't the only one who thought it would be impossible to write a book in just ninety days with a full schedule. I had told all of all of my potential clients about how my first book came to be, but it didn't seem to close the gap between their disbelief and reality.

That's when the idea first struck me. Maybe it was time to write my second book. I had known for a while that I was going to write another soon, most likely before the end of the year, but I hadn't set a plan in motion yet. I had spent the year working with authors to get *their* books done and stabilize my book-coaching business; a new book of my own never felt like a priority.

Of course, it would make sense for me to write a book. After all, I had based *my* business on the idea of using a book to grow a business. In hindsight, a second book was long overdue. Still, I wasn't completely convinced that it was my next move. I had two authors in my main program, and I was onboarding three more into the beta. On top of that, my next semester of college was about to begin in exactly one month. Did it really make good sense to go into another book?

I ended up talking about it with a friend whom I consider my editorial superior, and she pointed out that writing a book with all of that on my plate would actually be pretty serendipitous. You see, I was in the *exact* position that many of the people I was marketing to were. What better way to show them how easy it is than to write another book while running my business full time? It couldn't get more perfect. Although I had not consciously agreed to this new challenge, somewhere inside, I knew it was going to happen.

On July 28, I made a post on my social media profiles asking, "If I said I were writing another book in the next thirty days, what do you think it would be about?" This post got a lot of attention—more than I expected. Friends, colleagues, and prospects left comments and sent direct messages to tell me what they thought the book would or "should" be.

The responses ranged from sci-fi/mystery to meditation and spirituality. I think my favorite answer had to be that I should write about attraction and fashion. (People have known me as a "sharp dresser" for some time, and it would have been pretty on-brand for me.) While, ultimately, none of these were the book that I had in mind, it was great to see the engagement. That was when a light clicked on in my head (cliché, I know), and I saw everything so clearly—what my book should be, how I should write it, and how I could leverage it before I ever had it done.

Two days later, I was on a group call with one of my marketing coaches, talking about how my launch had gone. She nodded and smiled as I broke down my process, recounted my sales calls, and shared that I'd be starting two new authors in a

PREFACE | *xvii*

few weeks. There was so much positive energy in that space, and I soaked in the praise like a student whose work became an example of what "good" looked like. My heart pumped pride through every vein of my body.

I was so caught up in the moment that, before I realized what was about to happen, I said, "And you know what else?"

"What's that?"

"I've decided to write my next book. It'll be a simple guide taking readers through my framework. I've given myself a thirty-day deadline, *and* I'll be sharing the journey on my social media. It'll be great marketing and prove, beyond a doubt, that my method works."

"Wow, congratulations! I can't wait to follow you. We'll hold you accountable here in the group."

Just like that, the "plan" was in motion. I wasn't exactly prepared, but then again, that was part of why this was so perfect. Many of the authors I've worked with and set out to work with had little or no preparation. All they knew was that they were going to trust a process, and somehow, they would have a book in three to five months. If I trusted the process, I would have mine in just one—and by sharing my journey, I had built-in accountability. Knowing all of this, why not dive in headfirst?

On Monday, August 2, I got on Facebook Live and announced my plans. "I'm writing a book in thirty days," I said with gusto, "and I'm doing it while running my business full time, preparing for school, and making time for self-care." My friends and followers responded with enthusiasm. To them, I must have sounded like a magician announcing his next mind-bending act.

And so this book was born. With all eyes on me, I got to work the next day. At the time of this writing, it is August 15, 2021, and I have just sixteen days left in my challenge. If you're reading this, that means that I finished on time. As you proceed through this book, I hope you find every carefully chosen word and topic packed with value and that they stand as evidence of what can be done when you apply the right attitude, strategy, and implementation to your own seemingly impossible goals.

1

YOUR TIME IS NOW

"How to write a high-impact book fast?"
"Fastest way to write a book"
"Book-writing programs for online coaches"
"Best way to turn an online course into a book"
"How to find an editor"
"How to find a ghostwriter
"Should I ghostwrite my book?"
"How do busy entrepreneurs write books fast?"

If you haven't realized it yet, these are Google searches. Since you're reading this book, I'm assuming you've probably used a few of these yourself. If I had to guess, you're a coach, consultant, expert, healer, speaker, movement leader, or some combination of the lot, and you've been thinking about writing a book to grow your business or spread your message of growth, transformation, and healing. (If this is not you, then, you may have come to the wrong place.)

But let me back up. How did you get here? What drove you to seek, purchase, and open this book in the first place? Do you have a friend or colleague who published a book recently, causing you to consider your own authorial future? Did your new thoughts mysteriously turn into ads on your social media feed promoting a seven- or thirty-day book-writing program? (Seriously—*how* do they always seem to know what we're thinking?) Maybe you're more like my friend, Erin.

I met Erin in January 2021, through a mutual friend, Mollie, founder of Social Justice Kids. Mollie had found me sometime after I launched my book, *Facing Racism*. We had mutual social circles and similar hearts for change, and when I launched that book a few months prior, she decided we had to get in touch. We set up a video call to meet, and after almost an hour talking about the books we've read, the work we were doing, and the personal journeys that led us both to that moment, she invited to co-facilitate a Martin Luther King Day Virtual Conversation she was planning for parents and kids to discuss racial activism.

"You would really love it. These kids are so smart. Some of them will really surprise you! I'm also reaching out to my friend, Erin. She is just amazing. She would be perfect for this, but I don't know if she'll be available. She's so busy. Hey! I should connect you two. *She* needs to get a book out asap."

"OK, yeah. I'd love to meet her."

"You may have heard of her. You can look her up. She's done TEDx talks and run for public office."

"Wow! Please put us in touch. I'll try to make it to the event too." At that time, I had just made the decision to pivot from freelance editing to book coaching (which I'll talk about more in the next chapter), and Erin sounded like just the sort of person I would love to meet.

The MLK Day event was great! I only got to participate in the last half-hour, but Mollie was right on all counts. The kids did surprise me, not only in their social awareness, but their genuine interest in learning how they could act for racial justice. And listening to Erin speak was every bit as inspiring as

I'd hoped. She had poise, she had presence, and she spoke honestly. I knew from that thirty-minute segment, I wanted to work with her.

Near the end of the call, I sent Erin a private message in the chat. I told her how impressed I was by her and how much I appreciated the opportunity to learn from her even after I'd published my own book on the same subjects. I told her how Mollie said she was thinking about a book, and I offered to meet with her if she was interested. She replied, "It's great to meet you! Yes, thank you." We exchanged email addresses and I wrote to her immediately after the event.

We met through video call about a week or so later. She was at her favorite coffee shop, and I was in my bedroom-office. Just like in the MLK Day event, she was confident, but so very human. Talking to her felt a lot like talking to family. She told me a bit of her background: how she was bi-racial, adopted into a transracial family, raised in Europe, speaks four languages, and has spent the better part of the last three decades as a teacher and administrator at nearly every level of education imaginable. "Impressed" does not quite cut it for how I felt.

After running for public office, she used her digital platform to continue supporting her community. When George Floyd was killed and the country entered into another discourse about race, she didn't miss the opportunity to speak up about systemic racism, racial justice, and moves to get to equity.

Before long she was getting noticed and invited to speak and hold trainings based around her message. When the pandemic hit, and the country went into lockdown, much of her new work moved online. By the time we met, she was holding as many as *five* events per day, every week.

"You've got to be joking!" I said. "Five trainings a day? How do you manage all of that?"

"It's a lot!" She laughed. "Sometimes I get done with one and jump right into the next. It's a lot, but it's so needed."

"I'll say, it is. So, let's talk about your book idea."

"OK. Basically, I want to write a book that inspires people of all ages and backgrounds, something that tells my story in a way that captures what I teach in my trainings."

"I see. Have you tried before?"

"No. I haven't had a lot of time to put into it."

"Why do you think now is the right time?"

"People are ready," she said. "I'm ready. I've been thinking about it for a while now, and people have been saying it. I've reached a point in my business where it feels like my next move."

"What would you say has stopped you from writing to this point?"

"Well, like I said, time, for one thing. Also, I don't really know where to start or how to organize it. Is that something you help with?"

That's exactly what I help with! I thought. "I think so. If you had to summarize it in one sentence, what would you say you need the most help with?"

She thought for a moment, and then said, "I need a system. Honestly, I'm busier than I've ever been, so when I get done at the end of the day, I'm exhausted. I need a plan that I can work on that doesn't take up a huge time commitment but still feels like progress."

At that moment, I knew, not only could I help her, but that I *had* to. She was a passionate and committed to making massive change in and beyond her community. She wasn't just talking about making a difference; she lived her words every day. If she could inspire others the way she'd inspired me, she could make a real impact with a book—especially since her business was taking off, and people were looking for what she was doing.

She was mentally ready to write. She had a powerful message and knew it well. But a book was uncharted territory. It felt "big" and potentially overwhelming. On top of that, her workload kept her busy all day, and she wasn't sure how to fit a book into her schedule.

You may be like Erin: passionate, inspired, and dedicated. You built your business around making a positive impact in the world and helping real people transform their lives. You may have heard somewhere that you can make a bigger difference with a book. Perhaps you read an article about how a book can help you to build authority in your niche, attract premium clients, stand apart from competitors, and all of that.

Or maybe you've simply been holding onto the dream of becoming an author like a seed you're afraid to plant. In any case, that vision—the one where people are reading a book with your name on it and turning their lives around—has remained elusive for a number of reasons, like:

- Not knowing where to start your book.
- Not knowing how to organize your thoughts.
- Not being a strong writer.
- Having no clue how to tell your story in an inspiring way.
- Thinking that you need more experience before you have the right to publish.
- Having almost *no* time in your schedule to fit a massive project like this.

These are all reasons that I totally understand. Not knowing how to do something can be a major deterrent from trying it, especially when it directly affects your brand and reputation. And when you're already putting full-time hours into your work, it can really feel like there is no time left in your schedule for a project as intense and demanding as a book. If you're thinking that the road to authorship should not be taken lightly, I'd have no qualms in saying you're right.

Still, while these reasons are entirely valid, I've written this book because you and I believe (perhaps to differing degrees) that they are all hurdles that can be cleared. It's not a matter of if, but how. If these are your reasons for not writing your book, and you want to know how to overcome them, then this *is* the right place for you.

You see, a book that stays in your head is not making a difference for you, your business, or the people you've committed to serving. You're only here now because you know, like I do, that your time has come. You've been sitting on your idea for too long, and it's time for you to get up, to rise. Your audience is waiting for your unique message, and you are ready to deliver, even if you don't fully acknowledge your readiness. Often, the thing we must do, that we've been called to, is the thing we feel the least prepared for. If you've read this far into the book, it can only be because you don't want to let that list of reasons be your excuse for not showing up, playing full-out, and getting it done.

To make a long story short(-er), I shared my screen and showed Erin the ins and outs of my system. I showed her how each step was carefully chosen to take her closer to her goal and only required minimal time for maximum output. I showed her how the cadence was built specifically for someone in her position to be unable to fail.

She liked the way it sounded, and after talking with her husband, Erin messaged me to say she was in. *Perfect.* I set up her new project, and we began work on February 12, 2021. On July 22, just five months later, we published her book, *Bridges to Heal US: Stories and Strategies for Racial Healing*.

2

THE BOOK LIFE CHOSE ME

FINDING MY PATH

When you're new to the online coaching/entrepreneur space, it seems you meet a lot of people trying to do the same thing. I remember getting a friend request from a young man named Ryan, who appeared to be a book coach, like me. His tagline read, "I help coaches and entrepreneurs write short books to grow their businesses." Judging by the content on his profile, he seemed to know his stuff. I accepted his request and struck up a conversation.

Ryan was friendly and seemed genuinely excited to meet someone in the same niche. He asked a lot of questions like how I had gotten into the book-coaching business, why I had chosen this niche, and how long I'd been at it.

"Well, I pivoted to a coaching model this year, but I have been a writer and editor professionally since 2014," I said.

"Wow! That's a long time. Have you written any books?"

"Yes, I published my first official book last summer. What about you? How did you get into this work? Have you published any books of your own?" That's when I learned something surprising.

"Well," he said, "I just started book coaching about a month ago. I haven't written a book and I haven't had any clients for it yet. I was a marketing coach before this. Really, I've only been an online coach for about six months."

What? He has got to be joking.... Of course, he wasn't joking. Ryan was twenty-two years old and brand-new to this space. He had no background in writing, editing, or publishing. He had neither written a book nor helped anyone write one. Yet there he was, gallivanting as a book professional, likely giving us "real" editors and writing coaches a bad name. How could he possibly deliver results with absolutely no expertise?

Believe it or not, though, there are many book coaches out there who don't come from writing backgrounds. Many of them are actually business or marketing coaches who have written and leveraged at least one book. Don't get me wrong, I'm sure they have a lot of value to share! I bring this up because this is *not* my story. I actually had no intention of becoming a "book coach" or putting myself out there among a sea of digital entrepreneurs eager to carve out their new place in the post-COVID world. I started my career in the writing and editing space.

Let's turn back the clock. In the spring of 2013, I was in the middle of my second semester at Arizona State University. Through a series of unfortunate decisions, I was struggling miserably in my computer science major, and I had deduced that I was simply in the wrong field.

I went to see my academic advisor, who asked me what I would be happier doing. At first, I didn't want to admit that I actually hated comp sci because it meant possibly letting down my family and my friends in the Engineering school, but it was a truth that had to be accepted if I was going to make the money we were pouring into that school worth it.

"Honestly, I love writing. I've always loved it, and I do really well in English."

He told me I could switch to an English degree with an emphasis on journalism, literature, or creative writing. I thought, at the time, that the most meaningful use of my skills would be as an English teacher, so I chose lit. (Of course, I greedily took every creative writing workshop and editing class that my degree would allow.) This was my first career move toward a life that fulfilled my love of writing and my propensity for teaching and mentoring. I was already a tutor for my peers and a mentor in a writing group. By the end of my time at ASU, my editing instructors considered me "top of my class" and "ready to edit professionally."

In summer 2014, due to unfavorable tuition costs as an out-of-state student, I left ASU and relocated to Colorado, where I began serious work as a freelance writer and editor until I could find something more stable. "More stable" came in the form of a five-year retail career that need not be detailed here. What's important is that in this time, literary work was minimized, but not entirely forgotten.

In 2019, the Universe gave me hard signs that it was time to move on from my life in retail management by way of anxiety attacks, major health concerns, and a car accident. I took a leave of absence, flew to my childhood home in Southern California, and sat in the living room with my great-grandma watching game shows, reading poetry, and journaling. During this hiatus from my calamity in Colorado, I thought, *Wouldn't it be great if I could just do this for a living? Spend my days in the comfort of my home, reading and writing, and getting paid well for it... That is what happiness must feel like...*

That idea was a seed, and I had no idea it had taken such strong roots. I returned to my job in Colorado, and within a couple of months, my heart was made up. I'd spent long enough not utilizing my talents, ignoring my years of training in and out of school, and neglecting my heart's desire to build my own vision of freedom. It was time to go. I updated my resume and started applying for various writing and editing jobs—W-2 and 1099 gigs—determined to make it.

The Universe must have been waiting for that act of courage because my faith was rewarded almost immediately, with minimal effort. I landed a job as a developmental editor at a small publishing company, where I learned new skills and refined my knowledge of books and publishing. This is where I worked until July 2020, when the pressures of the pandemic lockdown forced the company to make some staffing changes. My contract was canceled, and I found myself freelancing full time.

Given my own literary and editorial background, it shocked me to see anyone professing to be a book expert without having gone through at least half the journey I had. Eventually, I realized that the edge these guys had over me (from a business standpoint) was the very fact that they *didn't* have writing backgrounds. They were living proof that one doesn't need a lifetime devoted to writing to become an author and make a difference. It all came down to understanding some core book-writing principles—the very ones I'll give you shortly.

BECOMING AN AUTHOR

In chapter 1, I mentioned that I published *Facing Racism* in 2020 (exactly one year before this one, actually). I'd like to briefly tell you a story about how that book came to be, as it pertains to this one's topic.

That book happened by accident; I never intended to write it. Rather, it was born out of a moment of inspiration that grew from conversations I was having on the internet following the killing of George Floyd. Like Erin, I found myself engaging the topic of racial justice and policing in new ways. I explained in that book that I'd actually been having a lot of "discussions" on social media that showed me I had much more to say than I had thought.

With all the emotional energy surging through my newsfeed, social media became an angry and vitriolic place. I wasn't sure if I had the energy to sustain an ongoing dialogue, and my initial sentiment was to simply pull away, to disengage from any discussion of race and George Floyd. I wanted to retreat to my comfort zone instead of pushing white Americans out of theirs.

Only, I couldn't. This was just too important, and as a young Black man in America, I had a vested interest in supporting the movement for change. How would history look at me if, in the moment of most-critical action, when my skill set was most valuable, I held back? I was armed with words that I knew could do something for someone. Soon, the idea grew in me that I needed to write a book.

I was still working at the publishing company at that time, and I let the idea slip to my supervisor during one of our meetings. "I'm doing so much talking on the internet, I could write a whole book about this stuff. I probably should," I said.

"Yes! You totally should. You would write a great book. You really challenge people, but in a good way."

It took another week or so before my head got on board with the idea, but inside, my soul already knew. I had felt the call, and I was going to answer it. It was not a question of *if*, but *when*.

On June 2, 2020, I finally gave in and started planning this book in the middle of the afternoon. I was staying at my great-grandma's house in California again, and I propped myself on the couch where, a little over a year prior, I had made the decision to follow my passion and live my purpose. There, I took my first steps toward authorship. I started with clarifying my purpose for the book. What did I want to accomplish? I certainly didn't want to position myself as an antiracism coach and start a business from it. No, I wanted to raise awareness and start a movement that people could carry on without me.

Next, I defined my audience and the book's topic and scope. I was going to answer one question: "What can white people who want to be better allies do to help fight racism in America?" That would be the fulcrum upon which the whole book would turn. Once I knew that, I planned my content—ten steps (eight after editing) to understand and overcome the roots of racism and prejudice personally so that readers could confront it socially.

The whole process took a few hours to really think through. I designed my book in a way that I believed could change lives. With my road map done, there was just one more thing I needed to be successful: a writing plan.

Back then, I was working a full-time schedule, helping at least twelve authors to develop their books each month. I had also taken on a couple of side projects and temporarily resumed my mentor role at an online writing forum I had frequented early in my writing and editing career. On top of that, I was helping take care of my great-grandma, who was ninety-four years old. So I knew I'd have to fit book work around all of those commitments.

It seemed like there really was no time for it. And honestly, there wasn't—not unless I created it. This was something that I'd said for a long time: we make time for what we want to do. If I wanted to write this book, I would have to create space for it. (I'll cover this idea in detail in chapter 5.) The thing was, I still wasn't sure I wanted to write this book. So creating space wasn't the issue I found myself needing to overcome—it was really deciding what this book meant to me and why it was important enough not only to fit into my schedule, but to prioritize.

Writing this book would mean finally accomplishing my

dream of becoming an author. I'd written so much and never published. I had helped so many authors to cross the threshold, but what about me, the devoted writer?

It came down to understanding how I wanted to view myself. Who did I want to be, and what did I want for my story when I looked back at my life? To me, the opportunity to be known as someone who meets the occasion in the moment—not after, not when it's easy and comfortable, and not when I could control the outcomes—meant more than being the guy who almost wrote a book. Would I have the courage to be the person I admired?

That's what my book was worth to me. It was enough for me to clear room on my schedule. If you're reading this, I invite you to think about what your book is worth to you (again, something we will revisit in the coming pages). Once I got clear on this, everything else was easy. I finished my manuscript on June 9, and the next morning I announced my surprise book.

THE ILLUMINATION METHOD

Now that you know a little bit about me, it's time to take a look at the journey we're going on together. To get a better understanding, I want you to think back *really* hard to your school days—probably to middle school or early high school, if you were an American student. Do you remember learning about "the writing process" for your essays?

The first step was always coming up with a topic to write about. In this preliminary phase, there was no real writing, only brainstorming and thinking about what we wanted to spend the next week or two exploring through our work. It consisted mainly of note-taking and talking in peer groups.

The second step was usually research. Since we couldn't be counted on as subject-matter experts, we were tasked with the challenge of finding credible sources and reading about our topics. At this phase, we usually had an assignment to develop an argument or thesis summarizing what we were going to say in our essays.

The third step involved some variation of making an outline for the essay we would write. We determined whether we would need five paragraphs or six, what the point of each paragraph would be, and what supporting evidence we would use for it. I usually found this step boring and tedious. I always thought, *Why can't I just write the paper and move on? I hate busywork....*

Then finally, after what amounted to 50 percent of our grade in "proper" prewriting, we had to sit down and actually write the first draft. This part came more naturally to me, and I usually did really well on peer reviews.

As an impatient student, by this point, I was tired of the assignment and ready to work on the next one. Of course, it was never that simple. There was the second draft, worth the last 25 percent of my final grade for the project. I was expected to take the notes from peer review and the teacher's initial grading and write a new draft. Then, and only then, was the paper considered finished.

If reading this felt exhausting, that's because that was my experience at the time. Back then, I thought I could just sit down, write my paper, and move on. It was only a grade anyway, nothing I cared about. Looking back now, I remember teachers saying that the subject and writing quality were not major components in the final grade. What mattered was that we understood and could follow the process.

But why was the process so important? As a student, I took it for granted because we used it so much. It became second nature, and I never realized that it would underscore my success well into adulthood. It turns out that this process is universal. If you write professionally, you probably follow some variation of this without really thinking about it. The reason is that it's a successful model.

Think about it. If you follow the steps, you front-load with knowledge before you ever make your first keystrokes. By the time you write, you know exactly what you're talking about, what you're going to say, where you're going to use concrete details and references, and how your document should flow to achieve your goal. Then, after you write, there is a built-in step to ensure that you said what you meant to say in the best way possible. It's no wonder we spent so much time learning to build this skill.

You have probably guessed where I'm going with this. Yes, you can use this *exact* same process for books, too. In fact, nearly every successful book goes through a version of it, whether that book is self-published or picked up by a big-name publishing house. The key difference is in how the process has been adapted.

When someone wants to write a book with a traditional publisher, they have to submit a book proposal. This proposal is composed of all of the details a publisher needs to determine if the author is serious and if the book has a shot at a successful print run. What most people don't consider is that this same document also has most of the information the author needs to write, edit, and market their book on their own.

There is lots of advice out there for what goes into a solid proposal. Every publisher and agent will tell you their way of doing it. In general, a few elements remain pretty consistent, and, if used correctly, a good proposal usually stops just short of being a blueprint to your book. See the image on the next page for a list of what these elements are.

1. Working Title _____
2. Hook or Tagline _____
3. Book Description _____
4. Target Market _____
5. Market Analysis (why your book is relevant) _____
6. Marketing Plan _____
7. Author Bio _____
8. Chapter Summary _____
9. Production Details (length, format, completion date, etc.) _____
10. Sample Chapter _____

Common Elements in a formal Book Proposal

These are not the only elements that could appear in a formal proposal, nor is this the only order in which you can put this material.

During my years as a writing mentor, tutor, editor, and now book coach, I've assisted dozens of authors at different stages of the writing or proposal-development process. About two years prior to this writing, I realized that there was some crucial overlap between the traditional writing process I had learned in school and that of creating a solid book proposal. When I pivoted into coaching, I had the thought, *What if I were to merge the two models into a single system that would give writers the keys to their futures as authors?* Thus, the **Illumination Method** was born.

In the remaining chapters, you will be guided through the ten core pillars of my signature Illumination Method—so named because of the way it illuminates authors to see their books with more clarity at each milestone. An adaptation of my flagship program, Illuminated Authors, this book covers all of the steps that I take my premium clients through when we work together, and it includes a few bonuses to help you be more successful as you implement this model for yourself.

THE ROAD AHEAD

In chapter 4, we'll look at how a book differs from other lead magnets, why people write and read books, how a book can help you, and your specific goals for your book. This may seem unimportant now, but it is a small yet crucial step in this process.

In chapter 5, we'll address the elephant in the room: your calendar. No matter what specific goal you want to achieve, you have to make room for it, and this is where you will learn to find the time in "no time."

Writing a book that matters sounds nice, but what makes a book matter to someone else? Chapters 6 and 7 are devoted entirely to defining and understanding your ideal reader (not to be confused with target audience) and to learning to write a book they will care about and want to come back to.

Every good book has some kind of structure. If you're going to write an unforgettable book, you're going to need the right content in the right order. In chapter 8, I'll show you the easiest way to organize your content, as well as how to structure your book for easy reading and maximum effect.

I opened this chapter talking about the generic "writing process." Unfortunately, despite a universal framework, there are elements of good writing that aren't so "cookie-cutter." In chapter 9, we will look specifically at *your* process and how to develop your unique writing plan. I'll share some key strategies to make writing easy and efficient and show you how you can adapt them to your own needs.

Once you get past chapter 9, you'll have a firm understanding of the foundations for writing any book. You'll know so much about your book that all that's left for you to do is write it. So, I've devoted chapter 10 specifically to writing. You'll get a clear picture of what to do and what not to do when writing your first draft as well as how to execute your plan for the best results.

Because no good book goes without editing, I've devoted all of chapter 11 to showing you how to edit your book, even if you're not an editor. I follow a comprehensive process, which I'll break down for you so that you can turn your first draft into something you're proud of.

With your manuscript written, it's time to learn about titling and outer packaging. Many authors waste time choosing a title before the book is written, but I've saved this for last because it is that important. Using the right language can make or break your marketing, and chapter 12 is where I give you my secret to choosing a good title, writing a description that sells, and designing an enticing cover (or choosing a designer).

Finally, in chapter 13, you'll learn about writer's block and the surefire way to get around it so you can maximize your time.

Each of these chapters corresponds to at least one module within my program. As such, I've added an activity to the end of some of them. The main point of these activities is for you to take action as quickly as possible. Many people read books and think, "That's good advice, I'll have to try that." Then they never do. I don't want you to fall into that trap. So the activities are directly related to essential tasks in your writing process.

WHAT THIS BOOK IS

While I was preparing to write, I found myself wavering on how exactly I wanted to deliver my message in this book. Did I want to be strictly prescriptive, like a standard "how-to" guide, or did I want to tell stories that could illustrate the points you need to know in a relatable way? Inevitably, I decided on both.

The best way to teach this material is to tell you what to do and show you how it works.

With that in mind, the rest of this book is a collection of strategies and stories chosen to give you a fundamental, usable understanding of the journey a book takes from inception to publication. I've loaded its pages with practical tips, personal experience, and client stories to help you overcome some of the most common hurdles that await you as a busy authorpreneur.

My goal is to help you match total clarity with the right plan so you can execute at high levels and get your book done. As an inspirational leader, healer, or entrepreneur, you've got a message of transformation that people need to hear. I understand that life and work can get in the way of big goals like this, so I've decided to keep this book focused specifically on the strategy and implementation. I wanted to help you answer the question, "How do I go from book idea to done and published with my schedule?" and send you off with the knowledge to take S.M.A.R.T[1]. action.

WHAT THIS BOOK IS NOT

This book is about taking clear, swift, decisive action. It assumes you already feel confident in your subject matter, your ability to do research, and the value of your personal story. As such, this is not a book about storytelling. I will talk about it—as no good book is complete without some story—but the focus is on getting through your draft.

Likewise, this is not a book to help you become a better writer. I assume that you have a comfortable command over the language you choose to write in and will be able to find professionals who can assist you with the "craft" of writing. We're going to cover so much that to throw writing technique on top would be both unhelpful to you and outside of the scope of this book. I considered including a list of books you can read to improve your writing style, but honestly, you've probably barely got time for this book, let alone five more (and the time it takes to practice).

This is not a memoir, and it doesn't teach you to write one. While I will use storytelling throughout the book, it is all in allegory to assist with learning. By the end of this book, you'll be able to write an effective self-help or personal-development book in a style that is authentic to you.

Finally, this book is specifically focused on crafting your own and does not spend time on marketing or monetizing it. That's a topic that could fill a whole book of its own.

As you read this book, you can rest assured that, while I could have loaded so much more into this book, I did not want to overwhelm or confuse you. I have given careful thought to what should be included to best serve *you*. What follows is the result of that. Now, with all of the formalities out of the way, let's dive in!

4

WHY A BOOK?

If you're serious about writing your own book, I think it's important to ask the big question: Why? Why take that step? Why now? What benefit does it have to you and your potential clients? To answer this, I want to talk a little about why people read and what a book actually is, especially when compared to other information tools and lead magnets. Then you'll start to get a clearer picture of why you're writing and what your book can and should do for you.

WHY DO WE READ?

Growing up, I loved reading and writing fiction. I was one of those kids with an overactive imagination, and whenever I read something good, I could literally see it like a movie in my head. Page after page, I would flip through books, embracing people who weren't there, adopting feelings that didn't belong to me regarding events that never happened in worlds that didn't exist.

It was all so real to me, and the lessons I took away from

each book had enough truth for me to see the real world more clearly. For example, the *Harry Potter* series taught me to choose my friends wisely—that status, wealth, and names don't mean much compared to loyalty and compassion. Another lesson the series taught me was the danger of inaction. "Indifference and neglect often do much more damage than outright dislike," Professor Dumbledore warns in *Order of the Phoenix*.[1] I could go on, but you get the point.

One thing you should know, though, is that I didn't read those books to learn—at least, not initially. I read them to be entertained. More than that, I wanted a full-immersion experience. I wanted to be spirited away to places where magic was real, friendships lasted forever, and problems could be solved by a band of kids with enough gall to stand up to "fate." This type of book captivated and inspired me. The challenge in fiction is to tell a good story that might also teach people something.

As a nonfiction author, you have the opposite goal: to teach something valuable and worthwhile and, hopefully, leave your readers with a memorable story. Readers will pick up your book and *expect* to learn. This is because books have been, since the dawn of education, an undisputed vault of knowledge. Let me conjure an image for you as an example. What comes to mind when you think of a wizard's study? Get a good mental picture, and then read on.

You probably saw a table or desk with a crystal ball. Perhaps there was something that looked like a chemistry set, too. In a corner, there was probably some strange animal like an owl, a snake, or something not quite identifiable. Scattered around the room—on the desk, on shelves, in towering piles on the floor—there were *books!* Wizards were admired not just for their skills in magic, but for the years of study and the volumes of books they'd read to build their magical prowess.

While humans have always been captivated by stories,

fiction didn't emerge until the early twelfth century—the novel as we know it didn't appear until about the 1700s, and it still was not the dominant writing form. It's safe to say that books have cemented themselves in our psyches as the ultimate learning tool.

Why am I sharing all of this? Because it answers the core question, "Why do people read?" Why would someone want your book? What value will it hold to them? In an increasingly digital world, where access to information is nearly limitless and people can get it in nearly every form, a book can seem like an antiquated resource.

This couldn't be more wrong. Because of our history with books, people still see them as the be-all and end-all of information tools. If someone wants to learn about a topic, they expect to get more in the pages of a good book than they would from a single documentary. While documentaries can summarize a lot, and podcasts can talk about a lot over time, they don't always provide the same depth and completeness that a book does. A book is prepackaged knowledge, waiting to be accessed, and readers can go to it anytime—even pack it up and take it with them.

Beyond content, it's also generally accepted that the very act of reading makes people smarter. I won't get into the science here, but if you search "How does reading affect the brain?" on Google, you'll find a plethora of articles, from people's personal reading journeys to science-backed health reports, listing the benefits. Some of these advantages include:

- Increased vocabulary
- Increased focus
- Reduced cognitive decline
- Improved brain connectivity
- Greater ability to empathize

Studies also suggest that reading can encourage better mental health by reducing stress, combating depression, promoting creativity, and improving sleep quality.

In short, people read books for self-improvement. For a self-improvement leader, having one's own book can be really attractive.

WHAT IS A BOOK?

Of course we all know what a book is physically: a collection of words detailing a topic in print, digital, or audio format. But what I'm really getting at with this question is what type of tool is it for readers and for authors? How does it work? What makes it work? (For the record, there is no inherent difference between a print book and an e-book. E-books are *not* inherently shorter than their printed counterparts, and I see no reason to choose only one format. If you write a book, you can publish it in multiple formats.)

Knowing that people will read your book to learn, you have to treat it like a learning tool. Where a book shines is that it gives you the space to go deeper into a topic. You get to flex your knowledge and showcase your experience in ways that you really couldn't in an onstage presentation, a twenty-minute podcast, or a YouTube playlist. It is a compendium of your experience.

Let's say that you're an expert bike assembler. You know every type of bike on the market now, all the parts they're made of, and how they've evolved over the last decade or two. Bikes are your thing and you want to teach me, a casual rider turned bike enthusiast (hypothetically speaking), how to assemble, fix, and modify any bike I buy.

You could write a twenty-page pamphlet covering the highlights of each topic. You could set up your own bike-building podcast. But you really want me to understand the science behind the latest bicycle technology. You want me to be well-versed in the tools I'll need and the different bike parts. It's essential that I know how the parts differ with different types of bikes. And you want me to be able to access all of this information in one self-contained, portable reference guide. A book can accomplish all of these goals.

What's more, I would expect all of this in a full-length book. If I wanted casual information, I would subscribe to a magazine. If I wanted entertaining bike talk with my Sunday coffee, I'd listen to your podcast. But I want to become an expert like you, so I'm going to find books that can teach me everything about bikes. This is how people think. To create a powerful product, you want to align to the reader's goal, which we'll talk about in more detail in chapters 6 and 7.

A book is also a statement to your audience that you are an authority on your topic. The general perception is that the average person doesn't just write a book. You have to really know a lot about a topic to be able to fill a whole book. And you must be truly passionate to commit so much time and energy to it. If you have a book that you wrote and published, it is your declaration that you have something to say that is valuable, fresh, unique, and well-studied (or at least well-thought-out).

This doesn't mean you need a college degree or accredited certification. You don't need to have spent years researching, conducting experiments, and collecting data. Your life experience can give you expertise in something. For our purposes, I'm going to assume you already have a niche that you know well. You've had your personal experience, you've done lots of studying, and you've helped or are helping people in your chosen space. If this is the case, then publishing your book can be a lot like accepting and asserting your role as a leader in your industry whom your potential clients can trust.

A full-length book, whether it's printed or digital, is

different from other types of lead magnets because readers' expectations are higher. If I'm being honest, there are a lot of books out there that under-deliver, and this does more harm than good to their authors' reputations. The ways a book can under-deliver include:

- Not teaching enough and being unusable
- Reading like an encyclopedia and being unusable
- Focusing on the wrong thing and being unusable
- Wasting too much time and being unusable
- Having poor presentation (editing and formatting) and being unusable

Notice a trend? A book's value is in its usefulness. Most "lead magnets" you come across are a collection of quick tips, short micro-trainings, and nonspecific information or tools that people can download on the spot. In my experience, they seldom contain enough information to be super helpful in the big picture. You may be thinking, "Well, what do you expect? The goal is to get you to buy their coaching."

Listen. A tool that can't be used is no tool at all. If you offer a useless product, how can your audience know your value? Why would they trust you if your first impression is underwhelming? Any lead magnet you create has to have value that the audience cares about, but you can typically get away with holding back a little in a five-page cheat sheet. You can't get away with an underwhelming book. Books are judged from the moment they get noticed, and unlike other documents, you have the space to over-deliver. Remember, it's never too much to go the extra mile. The fastest way to prove that you can help someone is to actually help them.

As such, and perhaps most importantly, **your book is a tool to help your reader achieve their goal.** Your reader wants a result. They have committed to learning how to get it. They've trusted you to show them the way. Don't hold back. I'll talk about this more in later chapters, but the thing to know now is that your book is not about you, and it's not for you. It is a tool to help someone reach a goal. You are the guide.

Ways in which you can over-deliver and exceed your reader's expectations include:

- **Creating a real, sincere connection.** Readers like to know they're learning from a real person. More than that, they want to know that the person writing to them actually cares about them. Take the time to show yourself.
- **Giving them useful information.** Avoid regurgitating the same information. You don't have to reinvent your niche or create a revolutionary new idea. You just have to provide a new take that moves your readers beyond what they can get online. Make it extremely applicable, not just theoretical or high-level. (Remember, you're helping.)
- **Providing encouragement.** It sounds elementary, but people like praise and support. Leave them feeling like they just learned a lot and make them *believe* they can get real results.

When you do all these things, you meet your readers' core expectations and needs. When you meet their needs, people like, trust, and remember you. This is the key to having a book that makes you **stand out to your audience** and **converts readers into clients**.

WHY ARE YOU WRITING?

Do you remember my story from chapter 2 about writing *Facing Racism*? Do you remember how I had to figure out what that book was worth to me before I could schedule and write it? Taking time to think that through really helped me get clear on what I call the book's purpose. When I take writing clients through my program, this is where we always start because it gives us crucial insight into exactly what the author intends for the book to do.

I firmly believe in the power of intention and visualization and how setting your intention before engaging in any major project can positively impact the outcome. I remember reading an article published by the *Research Journal of Physical Education Sciences*[2] that talked about a study done on basketball players. Basically, researchers gathered thirty male basketball players and tested their shooting skills. Then, they divided the players into two groups. In the control group, players continued practice as usual. The test group continued practice as well, but they were also trained in meditation and visualization. The experiment lasted six weeks, and then the players' shooting skills were tested again. Researchers found that the players who practiced meditation and visualization saw at least the same level of improvement as those in the control group. I had a similar experience when I was a track-and-field athlete in high school.

On a more practical level, when you clarify your intention, you bring focus to it. You actively decide what you want to do and what your desired outcome is. This brings clarity to your actions, allows you to measure progress, and allows everyone on your team to be absolutely certain of what "good" or "success" looks like.

Some things you'll want to clarify at this stage include:

- Who is the book for? Is it a personal project for your own benefit, or do you intend for it to help others?
- How will you use it? Will you be starting a new

business or pivoting your current one? Is it to bring support for a nonprofit?
- How do you plan to monetize? Does money matter? Do you care about profit from sales or will you be giving away your book?

This may sound really basic, but I urge you not to skip this step. Consider my experience. I knew without a doubt that I didn't want to be an anti-racism coach. I wanted to read and write books. I wanted to help people write. Anything else felt like a distraction. With that, I didn't include a call to action or any indication that I was doing this work with people. I also didn't spend much time promoting myself as an expert. Instead, I focused on sharing the book's message at a crucial time.

Erin, on the other hand, wanted a book that would support her business. More specifically, she wanted a tool that could take her message beyond her trainings and into the lives of more people. She wasn't concerned about money. That was coming from her work. She wanted this book to push her movement forward, tell her story, and provide her ideal reader with clear guidance to being the change.

My assumption is that you are looking to do something similar. You have to decide: Is this going to be a "for-profit" book or a "for-mission" book or both? Is there an upsell? Do you have a program or offer? How do you see this book benefiting you and affecting your life? How will your life be different after you launch? (Spiritually, materially, energetically, emotionally, etc.?)

Similarly, ask yourself these questions regarding your reader. What transformation are you hoping to encourage in them? What is your wish or hope for them? What outcome should they achieve after reading your work? How will their life change? Will they need more support? How does your product serve them?

Another question you want to answer is, "Why now?" Why is now a good time for you to take this step? What's changed from before and what makes now better than next month or year for you? Why is now the best time for your solution? Is there a need for it? Can you point to any studies or evidence of a problem that exists and how it may be underserved or how the current solutions may be ineffective? And lastly, why is your reader ready for your book? What would it mean to them to get the solution?

Finally, the last big reason uncovering your purpose is so important is this: you need something to anchor to when writing gets hard. You're going to be challenged. You're going to face writing blocks like imposter syndrome and things that come up at work. What about this project makes it so worth it that you'll commit to it even when other things come up? What makes it worth getting dedicated space in your calendar and in your mind? What makes it important enough to you that you will show up even when you don't feel inspired, aren't sure what to say, or aren't sure that you can do it? The person on the other side of your journey figured all of this out. They became the author.

ACTIVITY

This is a journaling exercise to implement what you've learned in this chapter. Either by hand or at your computer, open a clean page. Title it "My Book Purpose." Below that, write and answer all of the questions I've listed above (the bulleted and non-bulleted ones). You may not have answers right away, but the act of thinking about them will bring more clarity. I recommend giving yourself no more than thirty minutes for this exercise. You'll be able to add more detail later.

The point of the time limit is so that you don't get stuck here. You'll see time limits throughout this book because deadlines actually help you become more successful. People tend to take as much time as you give them to do something, especially when it's uncomfortable. With that, the first 20 percent to 50 percent is often wasting time. You want to take decisive action and move on.

5

CREATE SPACE

Do you remember how, when you first became an entrepreneur, you probably had visions of breaking away from the nine-to-five, creating more freedom in your life, and having more time to do things that you love? Now that you've been at it a while, you may have realized that running your own business is not as glamorous as people make it seem. You have to get up early and stay up late sometimes. You're almost always on call. If something is happening, you've got your thumb on the response button. You knew that you would have to put in some hours on your grind, but you probably didn't expect it to be this busy.

And that's the reason why you're here; you want to accomplish more, but time is one of your biggest hurdles. So that's what I'm going to address in this chapter. To be completely honest, if you can't get past this hurdle, you can't finish the race. Even if you hired someone to write the book *for* you, you would still need to commit some time for interviews, follow-ups, and approvals. (I'll talk about this a little more in chapter 10.) What I am going to do is help you to see what time you do or don't have and break some misconceptions that you and many others hold about your available time.

BUSTING THE "NO TIME" MYTH

I hear this over and over: "Andrae, I have been thinking about writing a book for a while. I probably have a few in me. It feels like something I'm supposed to do, but I can't find the time to sit down and figure it out."

First off, I totally get this. When you're busy with family, programs you've paid for, managing your growing business, and so on, a book can quickly turn into a far-off dream. Sadly, for many aspiring authors, the unborn book gets lost in "someday." To me, this is sad because the truth is, these people had *plenty* of time. They just couldn't see it. Let me give you a few numbers and you'll start to see what I mean.

Do you know how long it takes to write a book? Don't think about research or revisions, just the space at the computer between "Chapter 1" and the final "Thank you." No? About thirty hours. Yep, in thirty hours you could have a whole book.

Think about it: If you're really engaged with your material and can keep yourself typing almost continually, you can probably type anywhere from 800 to 1,800 words in an hour. In two hours of devoted writing, you would have between 1,600 and 3,200 words. A standard chapter is between 1,500 words (the length of a blog post) and 5,000 words. So, in two hours, you could write a complete chapter.

Many books are just ten to fifteen chapters. We'll call it fifteen for our purposes. At two hours each, fifteen chapters would take you about thirty hours to complete. Even if you took eight more hours, that's still less than one weekend! These numbers account for typing. If you dictate your book (using speech-to-text or some audio-transcription software), you can actually double your writing speed because most of us talk faster than we type (about 150 words per minute versus forty to sixty typed).

Now that you know how much time you need, let's look at how much time you actually have. There are 168 hours in a week, 672 in a month if you only count 28 days. (The average number of hours per month is actually just over 730.) You need just 4 percent of the time you have in one month. If you had eight weeks, you would have 1,344 hours, and you would still only need thirty (2 percent). If you had ninety days (twelve weeks; 2,016 hours) and the right plan, you could get your book done easily in just 1 percent of that time.

The problem is not that you don't have enough time. It's that you think you don't know what to say, and this is because you haven't been prepared. If you implement the strategies you'll learn in this book, you'll be able to write as expeditiously as I've outlined above. The thing to know about writing is that it is just one way of conveying ideas. You're thinking onto the page. What you need is a clear method of organizing your thoughts, which comprises all of chapter 8.

IF THERE'S SO MUCH TIME, WHY DON'T I SEE IT?

Still think there's no time for writing a book? I confess there's actually a small grain of truth to this. The thing is that there's actually no time for anything. There's no universal clock, calendar, or schedule that tells us what we must and must not do in a day or what we should and shouldn't prioritize. There's no one out there to tell us that we have to make time for one thing or another. There's no time *for* anything. We choose our activities arbitrarily. We tend to fill our time with what we think we want to do (based on what we've learned through socialization). Many things don't earn a place on the list.

Because of this, when we have big goals like learning a skill or writing a book, there's never any time in the schedule. We've already filled it with so many other things. If we were to stop filling the schedule, we would have a little bit more time. (Duh!) We can go a step further: if we were to pull things out of our schedules, we would be able to open up time. Now, I know what you're thinking. Everything on your to-do list is important. There isn't anything that you can pull out. That's okay. We'll look at your calendar shortly. The first thing we need to do is find the low-hanging fruit.

When I worked as a retail manager, there could be as many as fifty tasks a day, sometimes more. In order to accomplish all of them, I had to be able to prioritize what was most important, as well as what would be the easiest to complete. As soon as the store manager gave me my list of notes, the first thing I would do was look for the ones that would take minimal effort and time. Usually it was things like fixing the price on an endcap, sweeping the floor in the photo center, or assigning someone to refill a feature. These were the "ten-minute" notes, and when I set out to do or delegate them, I made it super clear to myself that they should take no more than five to ten minutes. They were the easy things that made no sense not to finish right away.

In terms of managing your time and opening up space, this analogy is less about completing tasks and more about finding the easiest areas to make an immediate difference. The first "fruit" you can reach for is wasted time. Now, I know it's hard to admit, but we all waste time. I'm not talking about those extra minutes that you took on a rare break, or that time you took to get lunch somewhere with a friend or your family. While those are "unproductive" uses of time, they aren't the most important at this level. What I'm talking about here are your habits. In what areas are you just giving away time?

For example, most of us use smartphones for almost every facet of our lives or businesses. We talk to friends. We conduct business deals. We interact on our social media. We do research. (In fact, since 2015, mobile searches have outpaced searches from desktop computers.) A lot of times it can be really easy to get caught up in these activities. Look at the time you start and finish each activity—and when you actually log out. Is there an opportunity to optimize this?

When I first started with social media marketing, I would spend hours logged in. Eventually, I had to ask my social media coach, "How long am I supposed to be spending on social media every day?" He told me about thirty minutes to an hour.

"Let me guess. You're closer to two or three hours right now, huh?"

He already knew. It took me almost an hour to think up, type out, and edit a decent post for Facebook (never mind reformatting it for other platforms). Then, before posting, I had to spend half an hour warming up my audience. Afterwards, I spent at least another half hour replying to people's comments and answering people's direct messages, trying to get sales calls booked.

Before I knew it, three hours would go by strictly on social media. That was time not spent doing any coaching or editing. I needed to find a way to minimize my social media time and maximize the output.

My coach was straight with me. "That's way too long, Andrae. What you should do is spend ten minutes warming up your audience, commenting on people's stuff, wait twenty minutes, then make your post. Spend ten to fifteen minutes responding to people's comments to help the algorithm, then come back around at another time in the day and get back to answering people who responded or sent you a DM."

Another way to optimize social media time, which I learned from my other coach, is batch-creating content. Throughout the week, I create a running list of content ideas that come up from conversations with my ideal client, topics that come up on my coaching calls, or ideas that strike me while I am working. At the end of the week, I take those topics and turn them into content for the next week.

Now, I spend maybe an hour or two writing, and then during the week, posting only takes about a minute since all I have to do is copy and paste the day's content. I give up two hours from my weekend and get back at least five during the week! That is a huge opportunity that could exist in your business. If not, *great!* But that's the type of thing you want to look at as low-hanging fruit.

If you're not so sure about how you're using your time, one quick way to find out is to check your phone's screen time usage. If you have an Apple device, then you should have a Screen Time app that will tell you exactly how much time you're spending on your device and which apps get the most of it. You can also check your battery usage, which will tell you almost the same information.

So you can see what I'm talking about, I've included real screenshots from my phone. These pictures show my screen time for the last week. As you can see, I've spent, in recent days, an average of eight hours per day interacting with my phone in some way. A lot of it was spent on social media—which makes sense because I was in the middle of a big marketing campaign.

CREATE SPACE | 41

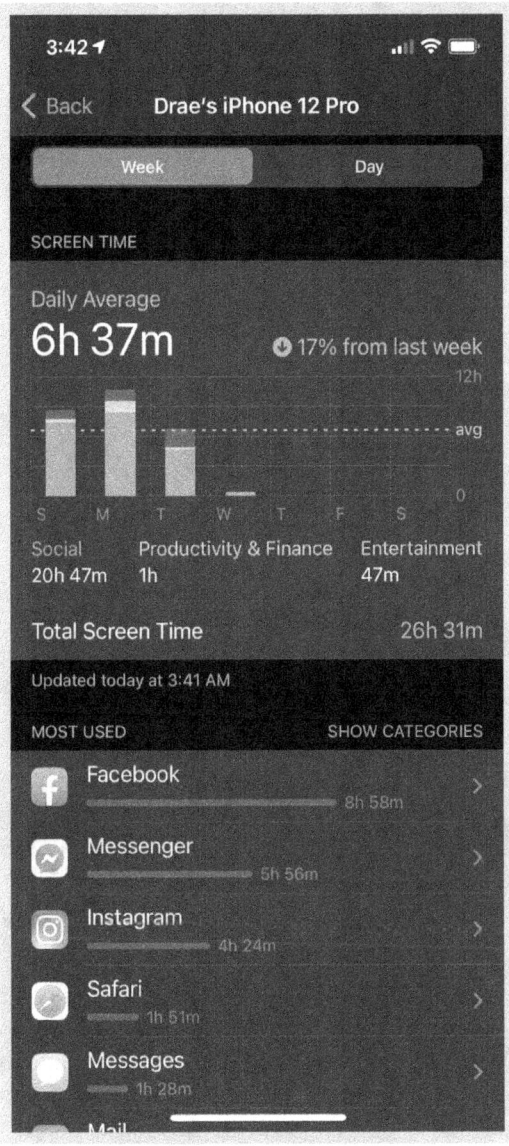

Screen Time app on Andrae's iPhone

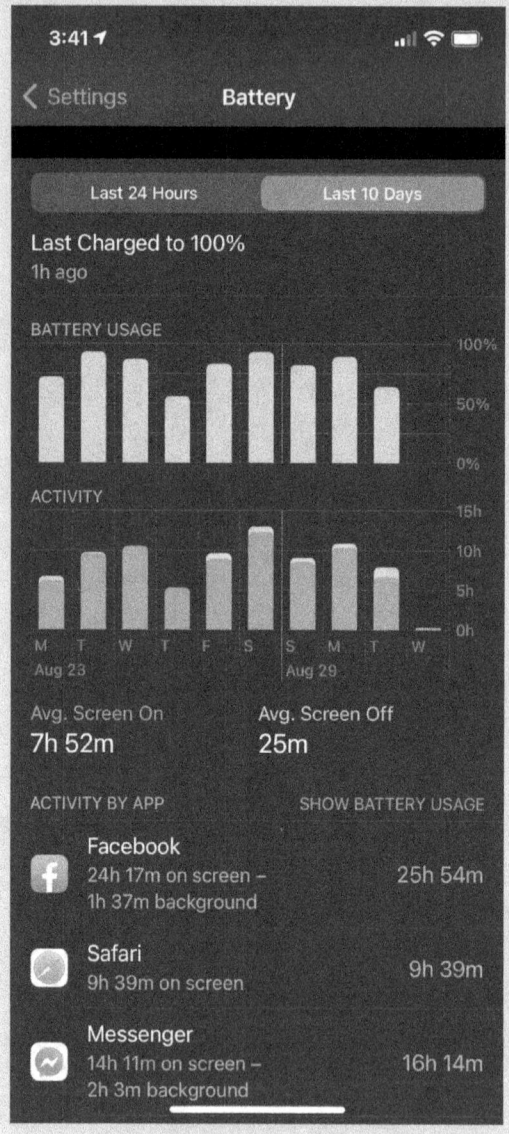

Battery Usage on Andrae's iPhone

LET'S take this low-hanging fruit concept one step further. While you're evaluating your social media time and your habits, one more category you want to consider is distractions. First, what are they? Obviously, in the social media space, there are memes, fan pages, friends' posts—all things that would sidetrack you from creating your content, replying to people, and moving on. This is what some would call being a consumer of social media.

There are distractions in the real world, too—commercials on TV, for instance, or shows that catch your eye when you should be working. Sometimes it's your family or a phone call from a friend you haven't talked to in a while. Now, I'm not saying that the people who are important to you are distractions. When I say *distraction*, I mean anything that steers your focus away from your goal and inhibits you from working toward your chosen purpose.

In this light, anything can be a distraction relative to the goal that you're trying to reach. If your goal is to spend more time with family at a certain time, your phone or book could be a distraction. If you want to create a post and get off of Facebook, that comedy profile or your friend's wedding photos may be distractions. If you want to get your book done, your work may be the distraction. This is where making decisions and setting boundaries becomes super important.

If you've committed to spending no more than thirty minutes a day on your social media, you've got to put methods and strategies in place that will allow you to get off at that time. You've got to avoid getting sucked into conversations, videos, and spaces that aren't supporting your goal. Double down on your commitment and practice discipline.

Another area of opportunity for boundaries might be in your business. For instance, meetings. I have a tendency to run over my time in my meetings sometimes. Even if the person you're meeting with wants more time, having hard stops is okay. You can always schedule in more time, but you don't want to make a habit of allowing people to test your boundaries and push you out of the time that you've allotted for an activity. This may not seem super important, but it can be a huge detriment if not controlled. Let me show you briefly.

Let's say that I have four meetings in a day, and all of them are scheduled for half an hour each. That's a total of two hours that I would spend in meetings. Now, let's say for three of them, I go over by half an hour. Those same four meetings that should have taken me two hours now take three and a half hours out of my day. What could I have done with that extra hour and a half?

In my experience, that's enough time to write at least one chapter of a book. Depending on how fast you write or the resources that you use, it could be two or three chapters of your book. Do you see how, all of a sudden, that time becomes so much more valuable?

As you can see, there may be opportunities for you to optimize how you operate in your business. This brings me to the next point. How do you handle urgent situations and things that come up in a day? Do they blow up your entire day? Do you push everything else to the side to make sure that you handle that one urgent thing? Do you stress out, panic, and become paralyzed? How do you emotionally respond to new stresses—how does that emotion impact your thought process and behavior?

This is an important piece because, believe it or not, our emotions actually impact our outcomes. (See the following image for a breakdown of the basic thought loop.)

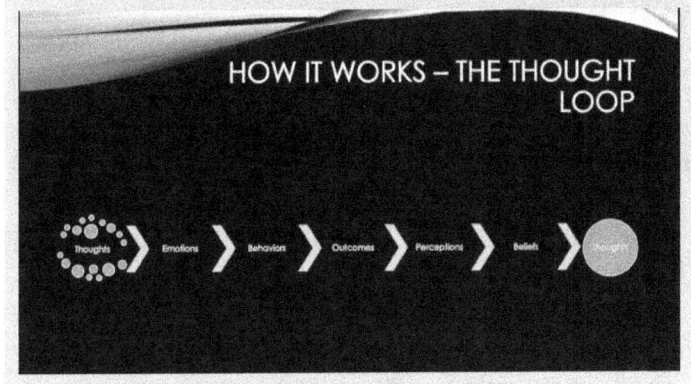

Diagram of a thought loop showing how thoughts are related to outcomes

IF YOU ARE FEELING EMOTIONALLY overwhelmed, the thought may come up that you have too much to do and there's no way you can do it all. That creates more anxiety and this negative feedback loop inside your mind and body. Instead of taking action, you find yourself stressing about having more to do. Once you've lost more time, you get paralyzed.

Have you ever been there before? I know I have. It makes you really want to avoid the thing you know you have to do because it becomes even more stressful to think that you might have to do more in less time. Avoid becoming overstressed and losing your cool when things come up. Things are always going to come up. How you handle them determines how long they're going to take.

BENDING TIME

Now, as promised, it's time to look at your calendar. Because you're a busy entrepreneur, yours is probably pretty full. Your day is probably scheduled from the moment you wake up to the moment you go to bed. Let's take a good look at what's on that calendar and how it's broken up. Is it all based on each day's needs, or is there a base routine that you follow? Let me explain the difference.

The first method is all about list-making. You start your day, you see what comes up, and you make a list of activities based around that. In theory, this can be pretty effective for task management. You can get a lot of things done this way. It was my secret to success in retail management. The problem with this method is that, in that job, success was defined by how many tasks my team could complete. Productivity was about completing more work, not necessarily opening up more time.

This is where the second method shines. It's about systemizing and optimizing so that every day you do your best work. As the leader of my own business, I cannot define my success by how many tasks I complete every day. Instead, my success must be measured by how well I build and run processes designed to accomplish the needs of the business *and* have time left over. (Remember how I said we tend to fill open time with whatever *seems* important?)

I had become accustomed to giving myself what essentially amounted to busywork that filled eight or more hours in order to feel accomplished for the workday. I never truly assessed what my business needs were and what activities I needed to focus on to make my business run. I was giving myself long to-do lists like the one you'll see in the next image.

Example of Andrae's "To-Do" list

If you look closely, you'll see there are things on that list like eating breakfast, checking emails, doing laundry, and following up on homework. It's not like these things didn't need to happen. They did. The problem was that I didn't give them a proper place within my life or work time and I started going through, trying to check as many things off as possible to *feel* productive. I rarely checked everything off the list though. A lot of things rolled over to the next day when I made the new list. What was the point of a list that never got *done?*

If this is you, I strongly suggest you break out of this cycle. The reason you don't have time for your book, or any other project, is that you have no control over the time you have. If you want to start creating space, you need to optimize your systems. For me, this meant identifying what is important. I won't break down my whole schedule for you, because that would be a waste of time (pun intended) but here is a basic rundown of what I did.

First, I classified my work into three categories: Administration, Revenue-Generating, and Service Delivery. I then broke that into a few subcategories:

- Admin
- Lead Generation
- Lead Nurturing
- Conversion
- Coaching
- Editing

Knowing the type of work I needed to do, I listed the specific activities I actually did for each and gave them a specific place in the schedule. For example, instead of checking my emails whenever something came up, I put clearing my inbox in two five-minute slots, one in the morning and the other in the afternoon. Posting content to social media and interacting with people got a thirty-minute morning slot. Coaching work got a one-hour spot after social media marketing.

As I did this, I started to notice more free space in the day. I also noticed that some work didn't need to be done every single day. If I wanted to, I could schedule all sales calls for, say, Wednesday and Friday between 3:00 p.m. and 5:30 p.m. If I set a specific time to reply to direct messages and decided on the number of conversations I wanted to have per day, I could do better pre-qualification, which could reduce the sales-call time too.

The other benefit of doing this is that it allowed me to figure out what operations needed my attention and which could be systematized and delegated. As the leader of my business, the writing coach, the editor, the marketing team, and the sales team, I was wearing too many hats. I would have to learn to let some things go and bring in some help. Which activities can you delegate in your business? Which ones need *your* attention?

I cannot stress the importance of this last paragraph enough. I learned the hard way just what it could cost to not have good systems and to bring on help too late. In the early days of my coaching program, I understood my service well, but I was still thinking like an employee rather than a business owner. In my case, the cost was thousands of dollars in refunds and extra expenses—all of which could have been avoided if I had understood the principles I'm telling you now.

Okay, getting back on track! Once you have your baseline work figured out, you can build in your flex hours to determine and decide the daily priorities. Every morning (or the evening before), have some planning time. Determine how you're going to move the needle forward. You can pick three to five meaningful focuses for the day. For me, this might be:

- Follow up on Author 1's cover design sheet
- Research ISBN batch pricing
- Stop by post office to mail signed books
- Record new videos for Modules 1 and 2
- Create outline for Friday training

The key is to do simple, meaningful work that has a

profound impact on your business. Don't fill your whole day from the time you wake up until you go to bed. That's exhausting, and you will hate yourself. Build in time for breaks. Choose a start and an end time for your workday, and commit to staying focused within it. The rest of the time is yours. Using this strategy, I opened about two to three hours per day that I could dedicate specifically to writing *this* book.

Now, what if your calendar is already optimized, and you already have a lot of extra projects filling up your space? Maybe you're launching a new program, and you've started a new mentorship, and you're a parent. How do you throw a book in there?

Do you remember how little time you actually need to write a book? Thirty hours. Let's add on six hours to incorporate planning. All you have to do is find thirty-six hours in which you can focus specifically on the one task of creating your book. That could be one hour a day for thirty-six days or thirty minutes a day for seventy-two days (just ten weeks). What is one way you can open up half an hour? Can you delegate an extra task? Can you choose to wake up a little earlier or stay up a little late? Could you shift some tasks in your schedule to different days?

Remember, if you've decided that writing a book is worth it, then there is room in a twenty-four-hour day for thirty minutes. Once you know where you can open space up, the last crucial step is to put your book onto the calendar. That's right, it's not enough just to have room. You want to write it in, just as you would any other dedicated task. This is your confirmation that this work is important to you, and it is also your official declaration of a designated time in which to do your book work.

This means that before and after this time-slot you don't have to think about it. (I know you will anyway!) During this period, though, everything else takes the back seat. Even if it is just thirty minutes per day, it is a focused thirty minutes, which makes all the difference.

ACTIVITY

This is a three-part journaling exercise. Take out your phone and review your screen time. Take note of which apps you use the most and for how long. For the ones with the most usage, write out all the things you normally do and how long you think those things takes you. As you go throughout your day, watch how much time you actually spend. Do you notice a difference? Where do you find yourself getting distracted?

The second activity is to look at your daily and weekly routines. Is there a sense of consistency? Write out all of the activities *you* do, how they serve your business, when you do them, and how long they take. This will give you a snapshot of how you're doing. You want to identify what can be delegated, optimized, or eliminated. You also want to take note of how many tasks you've given yourself in a day. Are you overloading with busywork or are you focused on work that matters?

Finally, pick three to five days out of the week in which you are able to reasonably open *at least* thirty minutes (preferably one hour) to working on your book. Then pick the times of day for each day in which you think you will be the most productive. Enter your book work into your calendar so that you can see it and receive reminders.

6

IDENTIFY AND DEFINE YOUR READER

When I started writing, I was an eager kid who loved telling stories. It was fun, exciting, adventurous, and a little rebellious. While everyone else was confined to the reality they could experience with their senses and the life they were born into, I had one extra dimension: imagination. Writing was a way for me to transcend the confines of what the world said was possible and start exploring all the things that allegedly weren't.

The stories I wrote were gifts from me to myself—not because I had no intention of sharing, but because I had no sense of audience. Each story was an experience *I* was invested in. Was I falling in love with my characters or caught up in the adventure? I believed that if it was this good to me, others would get what I was doing and enjoy my stories too.

This didn't really change until after my early college days, when I began my first writing mentorship. My mentor was a stern, shrewd woman who went by the name maia (no caps, no surname). She called herself the nitpicker-in-chief, and gee, did she live up to that title. Not only did she pick my grammar to death, but she was fond of telling me that my writing just "didn't make sense." maia was the first person to "teach" me about audience.

I remember I had just shared my latest piece of writing with her. It was a short story I had written for a fiction class at the university, and I got mostly good reviews from classmates. Ms. McNamara, my professor, said it was a "strong showing of [my] love for the craft," and her main critique was the believability of some of the middle content. You can imagine how eager I was to get maia's take.

Two days had gone by since I had sent it to her, and my fingertips were itching to start the revision. I checked my email almost every hour on the dot waiting for her reply. Half the day went by before I saw her message in my inbox. *Finally*. I opened it up and read it.

What I saw was not a glowing letter of praise for my improvement. I had learned not to expect that from her. Still, nothing could have prepared me for what she sent. She didn't like it. In fact, she claimed she couldn't read past the first page because it was "boring." She told me it read like an early twentieth-century novel written for an older British audience, and would never work in a modern American market. If I kept writing like that, I could get ready for a lot of unanswered query letters. More accurately, I may as well get used to writing for a trash bin because that would be my only audience. (Harsh, right?)

If there was one thing maia was good at, it was being "brutally honest" (a quality I hope to erase from the writing world someday). But when I really thought about what she was saying, she was never wrong. To make a long story short, we talked about it and her main critique was that the story would be uninteresting and unsellable because it was antiquated and dry. She asked me who my audience really was, and I told her I didn't know. I never thought about it. I just wanted to "write good."

She explained to me that not having an audience is great if I never plan to publish. If I wanted to share my work successfully, I would need to know who I was writing to. Full stop.

The audience determines everything from the message to the market. Even if my piece had been written to maia's standard of quality, not having a market makes it hard to pitch, which makes it harder to publish.

At that time I was writing fiction and had dreams of becoming traditionally published. Neither of these is true for you, but this story is just as important for you—perhaps even more so. Even though you're not pitching your book to a major publishing house, you still have the same goal of selling copies.

As a transformational coach or entrepreneur looking to attract clients to your business, you don't want to just sell copies, you want your book to be irresistible and persuasive to people who may potentially spend hundreds or even thousands of dollars with you. Who are those people?

Every successful book is written with a reader in mind. It has to be. Think about it for a second. If you're a man, which book would you most likely buy: *Get to the Climax: A Woman's Handbook for Better Orgasms* or *Peak of Pleasure: Understand Your Wife's Body & Give Her Better Orgasms*?

Probably the second one because you're a man. If you were a woman, you would likely be drawn to the first. The question you have to ask here is who do you serve? Are you a sex coach for men or for women?

Let's go a slightly different direction. Are you a sex coach for men over fifty or for women who've experienced sexual trauma? Or do you work with couples who need to reignite their passion after thirty years of marriage? Are they working professionals? Do they have children in the home?

All of this information seems arbitrary now, but I'll explain why it matters shortly. The bottom line is if you're in business, you serve someone. One of the biggest mistakes that I see new authors make is not clarifying their audience. They say, "Well everyone needs this, so my audience is everyone." While everyone may need your solution, not everyone is invested enough to be willing to spend money on you. If you're writing a book that transforms lives, it's only logical to ask yourself, "Whose lives am I transforming and in what ways?"

UNDERSTAND THE IDEAL READER

I opened this chapter talking about getting to know your audience. Your audience is the receiver of your message. In the standard communication model, there is a sender (you), a message (yours), a channel (your book), and a receiver (your audience). The audience receives the message through the channel.

As I pointed out above, though, not every market is a perfect match for your message. You want the audience that is most likely to see and respond to your message in a favorable way. You may know this as your target audience. If you were to write a book proposal and pitch it to a literary agent, they would be looking for that because that is how they determine if there is a sizable enough market to make publishing your book a profitable venture. As a self-published author, you'll want to know this if you want your book to make you money.

Knowing your target audience gives you a direction to cast your net (to use a fishing analogy... even though I don't fish). These are the intended receivers of your message. Many of them, if your target audience has been optimized, will be interested in what you have to say and may become followers or fans. But, as a concept, it is a little broad. What about the actual people in the target audience? What do you know about them?

You may be familiar with the concept of the dream customer or ideal client. In marketing, this is the person who would be a *perfect* match for your product or service. More than that, they have specific qualifications that make them the one person who would value your help the most and would be the most likely to take fast action if they saw your message somewhere.

I want to push this a little further to add that they are the person you wish all of your clients could be like. They show up on time for your meetings. They put in the work when you tell them what to do. They love you and you love watching them win (even if it's uncomfortable at times and you face resistance). You know that you can help this person and they know that you're the person to solve their problem. When you think of this person, words like "synergy" come to mind because you love working with them. On top of that, they are paying you your rates and getting real results.

What makes this person so perfect? Your dream customer is perfect because they meet a few key criteria:

1. They have a problem that you know how to solve. What they need, you have. You know beyond a doubt that if you worked together, you could help them get the result.
2. They know they have a problem or need and are actively looking to solve it. They have probably been trying to solve it for a while and are getting frustrated with what hasn't worked.
3. They would be prepared to take massive action right now if they found a solution to this problem. They have or can get the money and believe in your solution enough to start ASAP.
4. They know, like, and trust you. They relate to you and would reasonably invest in *you* as their perfect angel.

A person who meets all of these standards is someone who can be found, can be helped, would pay you for the help, and would more than likely do all the work to get the best results possible. As a note about point number four, this person often shares some or many of your life experiences. You relate to them on a personal level because you've been in their shoes and can understand their struggles and dreams at a truly intimate level. In some ways, they are you from a few years ago (depending on when you solved the problem).

It's important to target people with at least three of these characteristics. If you don't, then you may be missing an essential piece of the formula. For instance, you might find a lot of people with the problem. But if they aren't able or willing to pay you or are unable to pay you, they're not the most ideal. That doesn't mean you can't or shouldn't help them, but if you intend to make money, these clients would drain your energy.

You might find people who are willing to pay, but have a problem outside of your expertise. They think you're a close enough fit, but you don't know that you can get them the results they're looking for. You have to decide if they're worth taking. They may invest a lot of money to not get results, and then you will look like a fraud.

You might find people who have the problem and have money to spend, but aren't looking for a solution. You don't really want them either. You have to first convince them that they have a problem, then that you have the best solution for them. You're chasing, not attracting.

When you start thinking about using a book to attract your dream client, these are the criteria you should be thinking about because it makes sure that you position yourself in front of people you want to work with in your business. These are the individuals who you want to make up the body of your target audience. If there is one person like this out there, there are many more who are very similar. They likely have the same story or experience. They likely relate on an emotional level. They may have also tried similar solutions and not gotten the results they wanted.

Your dream customer is your most ideal reader. For the rest of this book, if you see these terms used interchangeably, just know that I'm referring to the same person. They are your target audience for all of your marketing *and* your book will be geared to this person and disseminated to your target audience of these people.

IDENTIFY AND DEFINE YOUR IR

Developing your ideal reader is a process I like to take in two phases: identifying and defining. I'm using both words deliberately here and want to make a small distinction between them for clarity. The *Oxford English Dictionary*[1] offers a few definitions to help us:

- Identify – *v.* **1.** establish the identity of; recognize **2.** indicate or select **3.** regard oneself as sharing the same characteristics or thinking as someone else.
- Define – *v.* **1.** state or describe exactly the nature, scope, or meaning of **2.** make up or establish the character of.

The key takeaway here is that identifying is a process of recognition while defining is a process of describing or characterizing. You want to do both because even though you may have a general idea of who your dream client is based on past clients, your goal is to clarify exactly who this person is. As I mentioned, knowing your audience means creating the right message for the right person, which is essential for a book that is going to make a real impact.

To start identifying your ideal reader, take a moment and

think about your absolute favorite client. Picture them clearly in your mind. Who is one person you loved working with so much that you wish all your clients could be like them? You may have a few people like this, and that's okay. At this stage, you're just identifying people you like.

Once you have them in your head, take out a piece of paper and start listing all of the things you loved about this person. How did you meet? How did they decide to hire you? How old were they? Where did they live? What were they struggling with? What was the process of getting them into your program like (easy or difficult)? What was their life like before they met you? What was it like to work with them? What did you learn about them through the coaching?

Think of as many things as you can and write them down. This is the foundational information you'll need to actually define your ideal reader. You want to use as much of this real "data" as possible to make a more complete and lifelike snapshot.

The point of this information is to start building your dream client avatar. You may have heard this term before, but I want to recap briefly. You can think of it like this:

Imagine you've just bought a new video game and your first step is to create a customizable character. You input information like height, weight, skin color, body type, hair length, and voice. If it's a fantasy RPG (role-play game), you can choose the race and job class too. You select your specific skills and weaknesses and perhaps even what realm you're from. The more information you input, the more realistic this character becomes. (A few games even let you pick your quest and backstory.)

That character is essentially an avatar for you to interact with the game world. It is a data-based composite of various character traits you defined at the beginning of the game. We can apply this concept to the dream client avatar. You want to provide as much information as possible so that this avatar feels like they are or could represent a real person.

The information you need isn't as trivial as in a video game, though. You'll want to know everything about that person's life, struggles, desires, longings, beliefs, challenges, and background. If you use the right information, this avatar will allow you to see into your dream client's psychology and understand them better than they may understand themselves. This is what will allow you to create a book that feels tailor-made for your ideal reader and a marketing plan that attracts them.

When I wrote *Facing Racism*, this was one of the first things I needed to do in order to unlock my book's potential for sales and impact. I started with basic information and demographics:

Name: Jeremy Boyd
Age: 38
Location: Redlands, California
Job: District Manager Restaurant Chain, volunteer coach
Family: Wife who works part time as a substitute teacher, four kids
Demographics: Middle class white male. Doesn't think of himself as privileged. He has a younger brother who is single and a younger sister who married a black man and has two kids with him. Jeremy's Dad is in the Police Department, his uncle works for the Fire Department, and his Grandfather was in the Air Force, so he has mad respect for servicemen.

This basic information seems nominal, but it gives me a general sense that this is not just some vague idea but a real person. I could find a district manager in Redlands. I could find someone whose family is in public service. I can understand the challenges of a middle-class American in the suburbs trying to raise four kids. Perhaps most importantly for my book, I could understand that, with his niece and nephew being biracial, there's no way Jeremy would think of himself as racist. Are you starting to see the usefulness here?

The next thing I did was ask some targeting questions to help me better get into the mind of my new character and think about where I might find him. (This is all about positioning.)

1. What does your ideal reader do for fun?
2. Where does your ideal reader shop?
3. What does your ideal reader watch on TV or search on the internet?
4. What types of books, magazines, or blogs do they read? (What are they reading right now?)
5. What are some hashtags that your ideal reader follows on social media?
6. Who are five influencers, figures, or profiles that your ideal reader follows (i.e., Oprah, Michelle Obama, Russell Brunson, Warren Buffett, etc.)?
7. What is most important to your ideal reader? What are they passionate about?
8. Do they already have or follow coaches? Who? For what areas of their lives?
9. Do they listen to podcasts? Watch videos on YouTube? Join Facebook groups? Follow trends on LinkedIn? If so, which ones and what specific podcasters, channels, groups, and trends?
10. What area of life are they struggling with right now? What problem are they trying to solve that you help with?
11. Why do they feel that now is the best time to solve this problem?

Answering these questions was not easy. They really made me think about the real people I *wanted* to read my book and where to look for them. I realized a major distinction about my ideal reader at this point. While I initially believed I was writing to someone who really didn't understand racism or the conversations that were happening, it became apparent that my ideal reader was someone who was actually more open to conversation. They wouldn't be heavily conservative or against talking about racial justice, but probably more moderate and leaning toward liberal.

My readers would probably be corporate leaders who needed to improve DEI efforts in their organizations. They would probably be looking for books and speakers to help them understand this complex social dilemma.

You do not have to ask these specific questions, nor do you have to answer all of them, but you want to have some targeting questions to really flesh out this person.

The final piece of this puzzle is to write a bio or profile for your new avatar. In this bio, you really want to avoid the basic demographic issues and dig into the heart of who they are, what they believe, and what their life looks like through their eyes. It is important to establish their worldview, their present understanding of their problem *in their words* as well as what they think they need.

This bio should read less like a short story and more like a personal interview. Imagine you're your ideal reader, and you've just been asked to talk about your life and what you need help with. Then tell us about yourself in first person. You can think of this like acting or role-play. You're not describing them; you're tuning in and *becoming* them. Here's what I wrote for Jeremy:

> My name is Jeremy Boyd, and I work as a district manager at Subway. I've been in this job for a few years now, and I enjoy the freedom and mobility it gives me. My wife, Stacy, and I have four kids: one daughter

(Kimmy) in high school, two boys (Chase and Jason) in middle school, and one more boy (Jackson) in elementary. Stacy is a part-time substitute teacher for elementary. It's very fulfilling for her, and I'm glad she's able to do something she enjoys. She's never been one to stay at home, so I love that she can still be at work, even while taking care of our youngest.

Me and Stacy do our best to keep food on the table and give our kids a good life through honest hard work. We believe you get what you work for, and we teach our kids to work hard for what they want. Now that Kimmy is in high school, though, we're trying to figure out how to pay for her college. We aren't rich, but I'm pretty sure we make too much for a ton of federal aid. It's a little disheartening to think that, thanks to things like Affirmative Action, my oldest might get looked over for scholarships and financial aid because she's white. But I push her to be her best anyway. I get that minorities need a little help.

Now, I'm not racist. I love African American people. All people, really. I just think everything should be equal. I'm very upset about everything that's been going on in the news with the protests and the riots. I get why people are upset, though. My dad's a cop and my grandfather served in the Air Force most of his life, but I don't think either of them would stand for the killing of any unarmed citizen.

It's disgusting what happened to George Floyd and so many other African Americans. I never thought it was racially charged and I think we definitely have a problem with a few bad apples ruining the police reputation and

IDENTIFY AND DEFINE YOUR READER | 65

abusing their power... but I can't really ignore what's happening. It's getting clearer that we still have a racism problem in this country and, if what happened to George is really happening to other people, it's sick.

My brother-in-law is African American and my niece and nephew are mixed. It scares me to think that any of them could be in danger just because some punk with a gun has a problem with how they look or the music they like! Kimmy's best friend, Jazmin, is Black and they hang out all the time. Or at least they did. Kimmy's afraid that all this hatred and stuff will ruin their friendship. I coach Pop Warner football for my son's team as well and we have kids from every race. They're all great, with bright futures and big dreams. They don't see color, and I hope to keep it that way.

I think that's wrong, that our kids are or will be affected by all of this. They didn't ask for this problem. It makes me mad, thinking that people can be hateful like that, and me and Stacy want to raise my kids better. I'm starting to see that I, as a white man, have to step up and do something if I want to make a better world for them. The problem is, I really don't know where to start. We have doubled down on anti-racism policies at work, but I want to do more. I don't think changing a few policies is enough to make lasting change. What's to stop people from doing things outside of work?

I know I don't fully understand the problem and can't totally grasp what Black people must be feeling, but I want to be a part of the solution. I never thought of myself as a part of the problem, but I believe in freedom and standing up for what's right, and I have to make sure my kids can have the same freedom that my grandpa fought for. I don't want them to be afraid because of who they love or hang out with. I don't want them being singled out because they stand up against violence and hatred. I need to know how I can do more to fight racism for good and support the future of my mixed niece and nephew.

Creating a bio sounds superfluous and time-consuming, but it can be both fun and insightful. You see, everything you say as your avatar is based on what it feels like to walk in their shoes. It forces you to think how they would think. This is how you go from having an ambiguous target audience of people in a similar age range to an optimized audience of people who are the best fit for you!

I KNOW I've spent a ton of time talking about the ideal reader. That's because this is the most important part of this process. Your ideal reader is the key to your entire book. The topic you choose, the content you include, the way you organize your chapters, and the marketing language you develop all stem from your ideal reader. The better you understand them, the more accurate you can be in your book. The more accurate you can be, the more quickly and effectively you can write, publish, and promote.

The last thing I want to remind you of is that you've probably *been* your dream customer at some point. Somewhere in your past, you had a problem that you needed to solve. You were desperate to solve it and tried everything you could to figure it out. It wasn't easy. You may have reached your wits' end and thought about giving up. Then, as if by fate, a small window opened up, and through it you discovered the key and experienced the breakthrough that changed your life forever.

Your ideal reader is you before the breakthrough. They are looking for an answer. They need to find it. They can't keep living the way they are now, and they know it. They're waiting for someone (you) to open a door.

You love them not just because they're going to spend a lot of money with you. Not just because they'll get results in your program, either. You adore them because you can relate to their story. There is a connection deep down, and if you can tap into that, you will be able to talk to your ideal reader like a real person who needs your help. You have to have a passion for helping them.

ACTIVITY

Now that you have a thorough understanding of your ideal reader, it's time to put this into practice. Wherever you are taking notes, start a new page titled, "Ideal Reader." Using the examples I've provided previously as your guide, start identifying and defining your ideal reader for your intended book.

If you've been successfully running your business and attracting your dream clients, you may already have *all* of this information stored somewhere. If so, you can copy and paste it into your document or copy the file into your book's project folder. You don't need to do double work. The important thing is that you have this information in mind as you move forward.

7

CHOOSE YOUR BOOK'S TOPIC

So far, we've talked about the "why," the "when," and the "who(m)" for your book. Now it's time to look at the "what." Every book has a topic. This topic is essentially your focus, the nexus that connects your ideal reader to your subject matter.

Because I am a true word nerd, I want to make another distinction here. What is the difference between "topic" and "subject"? This may seem arbitrary—and in a practical sense, it is nominal—but for our purpose, it will be useful to understand this before moving forward.

A subject is defined in the *OED* as a "branch of knowledge studied or taught in school." A topic is defined as "a matter dealt with in a text or discourse." Put another way, your subject is the area of knowledge that you pull from, whereas the topic is one specific aspect of that which you've chosen to focus on in your work.

For instance, if you are a financial advisor, your book's subject may be something like personal finance. If you wanted to get more specific, you could niche that down to areas like investing, banking, and retirement planning. None of these are quite specific enough to be a topic, though.

Your topic might be something like, "how to start planning for retirement in your mid-twenties" or "how to achieve financial freedom through smart investing" or "how to create a healthy financial portfolio with as little as $1 a day." Do you see how all of these are within the subject of personal finance, but they are each specific to one aspect of that area? Your subject is like your genre, but your topic is what *your* book is about within that.

Where I see most new authors go wrong is that they never actually choose a specific topic. They think "financial planning" is the topic, but because it's so broad, it poses problems for them as the author and for readers. What's most likely to happen is you'll start thinking of all the things you could teach, and then you'll realize you have no clue what should actually be included. You'll feel yourself getting stuck trying to figure it out, and you'll file your book away to come back to "when you have more time."

If you manage to avoid this pitfall, you've probably addressed it by choosing five to ten things you *think* everyone needs to know about your subject and deciding that those will be your book. This may or may not be useful or interesting to anyone but you and other professionals in your field. When it comes out, the book will read like a compilation of your experience in your field rather than a book that means anything. I classify this type of book as a "reference guide" because that's how people tend to treat these sorts of books (at best... at worst, they are placeholders).

One thing you need to understand is that, if the ideal reader is the key to your book, the topic is the doorway. It gives you and your readers a way into the material, making it accessible. Choosing *one* specific topic allows you to stay focused and relevant, which increases the potential impact of your book. Think about it: if you write about five topics in one book, can you really go deep into any of them?

All of this points to this chapter's central question: How do you choose a good book topic? If you're like most new authors, you probably came into this program thinking you knew exactly what you were going to write. Now, I'm not here to say that you can't write that book. But it's important to understand that since everything is relative to your ideal reader, you have to write a book that they're going to want. You have to write about a topic that your readers are interested in buying.

What are your readers interested in buying? Solutions to their problems. People pay money to solve their problems. So if you want to write a book that reaches your audience, helps your clients, and grows your business, you have to write a book that solves a problem. This is the foundation of the self-help genre. Someone has a specific problem (or needs to reach a certain goal) and they seek a book that will help them solve it. I call this problem your *reader's specific problem*, RSP for short. Your book will be positioned as the solution.

Knowing your reader's specific problem makes all the difference between writing a book that makes readers fall in love with you and one that gets treated as general reference. The former is results-oriented. Your book is designed to help the reader solve this specific problem. Everything you include will be framed so that the reader moves steadily from problem to problem-solved with every chapter.

This actually reminds me of an author I worked with named Tyler. Tyler was a successful entrepreneur who had built over four six- and seven-figure businesses and who had helped a number of people to start their own. His next move was to pivot into coaching, and his book was going to be a part of his marketing plan. When it came time to choose his topic, he thought his topic was building, growing, and running a successful business.

"I understand that's your strength," I said to him, "but that's really broad. It would make your book long and unfocused."

"But that is what my readers want to be able to do," he said.

"In the long-term, yes. But think about where they are right now. If they wanted to know all of that now, why wouldn't they have bought any of the other books out there?"

All of this was via email, and so it took him some time to get back to me. Finally, when he did, he said, "I don't think my reader is confident enough to do it yet. Thinking back to when I was starting out, becoming a seven-figure CEO sounded intimidating and unrealistic. I just wanted to get my business off the ground."

Tyler didn't realize it until later in our conversation, but he touched on a very critical point. *His* ideal reader was someone who wasn't ready to think about becoming a major CEO. They were someone who knew they wanted to start their business and just wanted to be successful at it. Once we knew that, we had an access point and a focus for his book. Everything that went into the book was measured by its relevance to that specific goal. By not including anything else, Tyler had more room to talk about this topic and pack the book with value. (It also left room for him to deliver more in other books and coaching.)

There's another reason why identifying the RSP early on is important: marketing. The reader's specific problem corresponds to the words your dream customer would be saying at the point just before they are ready to buy. If you centralize your marketing language around that, you're going to get noticed. Let me give you a new example.

Let's say that you are a doctor and you specialize in gut health (since this is a trendy topic right now). You take a lot of clients who come to you with stomach cramps. When you see them in your office, are they saying, "Hey, doc, I need you to help me heal my gut," or are they saying, "I really need to get rid of this stomach pain"? The latter statement represents what most people would naturally say. You as the doctor would know that they probably need to heal their guts.

You can't publish a book that says, "Heal your gut today!" if you want to attract readers who are coming to you about stopping their stomach pain. They wouldn't recognize your book as being for them compared to a book that says, "Stop the Stomach Pain for Good!" You want to be positioned as a problem-solver, not just some expert. You want to be the expert—the perfect person to help your dream customer. The cool thing is that you test this out on people who match your avatar and get market validation.

There are two ways to develop your reader-specific problem. The first is to go over any notes pertaining to real clients you've helped who match your dream client avatar. Hopefully you saved their intake forms, application questions, and coaching call notes. If you did, all you have to do now is look for what they said their problem was. What did they say they were seeking help for? Don't confuse this with what you *actually* helped them with or the real thing that was holding them back. You want to home in on what they were aware of before working with you because that is what they were looking to solve and willing to invest money into.

The second option is to refer back to your avatar and bio. If you did the exercise right and got into character, your bio should be *loaded* with language that you can pull from. Tyler and I reviewed his avatar and, sure enough, just as Tyler had said, his dream customer described himself as a budding entrepreneur—someone who wanted to get his new business off the ground and stabilized. This ideal reader had tried starting his own businesses before, but they always failed within a few months, and he really wanted his next to be a success so that he could one day stop working his dead-end nine-to-five. So Tyler's book became about helping new entrepreneurs go from clueless and stalled to confident and successful. (For confidentiality reasons, I have intentionally omitted the name of Tyler's book and any identifying information.)

The other half of the book topic equation is your ideal reader's heart's desire—RHD for short. Remember that people are typically running away from something or toward something. If they are running from their problems, then they likely have a vision of what they do want instead. This is what your ideal reader thinks their life will be like, if they got the problem solved. What's on the other side of that problem? This is important because this is the vision that your ideal reader is holding—solution in their mind. The dream come true is basically the reader-specific problem solved. So if your ideal reader comes to you saying, "I need a way to stop the stomach pain, but my doctor isn't listening to me," the RHD would be, "My stomach pain is gone and I feel better than ever."

Let's take a look at a couple of books that are on the market now and see if we can identify the RSP and RHD on the cover. These are books that I have on my bookcase, chosen at random. I had no involvement in these books. I'm merely using them as illustrations to point to the fact that this concept is evident in books well outside the ones I help my clients write. The first book I have pulled is Gary Chapman's *The 5 Love Languages: The Secret to Love that Lasts*.

From this title and subtitle we can guess that, more than likely, this reader's heart's desire was something like, "I found a love that lasts" or "I know how to make my relationship last longer." From that we can infer that the reader's specific problem was something along the lines of, "How can I make my relationships actually last?" Here is a world-famous book, a pillar in the relationship advice category, and it is using the same formula to attract and serve readers across the globe.

Another book to consider is *Destiny: Step into Your Purpose* by

T. D. Jakes. From this title and subtitle, we can infer that this ideal reader is struggling to find their purpose in life. So the heart's desire is probably something along the lines of "I know how to find my purpose" or "I know how to live my purpose."

Hopefully you're starting to see how, together, the reader's specific problem and heart's desire become the foundation for all of the marketing language. Your ideal reader will see it on the cover of your book and know, instantly, that your book is the right one for them. After reading your book, they'll know that you are the right person to solve their problem because of how you focused and structured your content. On the Thank You page at the end of this book, I've included a link to a **free** worksheet that will help you to get super clear about this.

Before I close out this chapter, there are just two small steps that I would like you to know about. While they aren't essential to understanding the scope of your book, taking them will help you to quickly articulate what your book is about to your audience.

First, once you have your problem and desire, try boil down your topic to a "how-to" one-liner. As an example, consider the RSP for this book:

RSP: I want to write a quality, meaningful book for my coaching business, but I don't know how to do it while still working my full schedule.

RHD: I know how to get my book done quickly.

My topic one-liner for this book would be, "How to write a high-impact book for your business with a busy schedule." Sounds familiar, right? This became the foundation of the book's subtitle. This won't always be true, but the two will often be closely related.

The final step I encourage my authors to take is to derive their one-sentence elevator pitch from this. The structure of this should be loosely based on something like this: "My book helps [description of ideal reader] overcome [specific problem] so they can [achieve heart's desire] without [thing they want to avoid]."

Taking the above, my simple pitch would be, "My book teaches coaches and consultants an efficient writing system so they can finish their nonfiction books without confusion and overwhelm." Pretty clear, right? Whenever someone asks you what your book is about, you'll want to use some form of the one-liner or the elevator pitch because it is optimized to be attractive to your ideal reader. Any time they hear it, they will become instantly curious.

So there you have it, your book topic explained. To briefly recap, your book topic is based around your ideal reader's specific problem, which becomes the fulcrum of your book. Coupled with the reader's heart's desire in their words, it forms the basis of all of your marketing language too. If you take the time to get to know these two things, they will not only make it easier to attract clients, but it will also make it so much easier for you to decide on the scope of the book. In the next chapter, we'll look at how your topic impacts the content and organization of the book.

ACTIVITY

For this exercise, review all documents pertaining to your ideal reader, either your work from previous chapters or from your case studies and files. Take note of what your real clients have said about their problem. Compare and contrast this with what is in your avatar. Then use the bonus documents from the Thank You page to determine your book's topic. Remember, the book is about solving your reader's problem, not showcasing your knowledge. The fastest way to prove that you can help someone is to actually help them.

8

STRUCTURE AND CONTENT

"Writing your book should be fairly easy," I said.

"Okay..." my dad said.

"Do you doubt me?" I smirked.

"No, son. It's just a little hard to wrap my mind around. I want to be able to tell my story in a way that helps someone. But there's a lot of stories to tell. I'm not sure people want to know *everything*."

"You're right. They don't. But that's actually what makes it easy. We don't need your whole life story—just about twelve or so good stories and the lessons you learned. We can choose the ones that are most relevant to your reader right now, and there's your book."

We were sitting across from each other at my dad's dining room table. I was staying with him for a few weeks in California before the state went into lockdown. It was the first time in our lives that he had a place entirely his own where he could host me. After years apart, some force had brought us together as if no time had been lost, and instead of one of us resenting the other, we were planning his book.

My dad is a musician and built his life and legacy as such.

He spent much of his youth working in his dad's appliance shop and playing the organ in the church that my grandfather pastored. Due to turmoil at home, my dad ended up being homeless as a teenager and never finished school beyond the sixth grade. All that to say, he was never exposed to the writing strategies that one starts learning in seventh grade and on—the ones that I've built my career around. To him, this was entirely new territory.

"You can think of your book this way," I said. "It's going to have three parts: an intro, a body, and a conclusion. Each part has its own goal. Since we know what your reader wants, the goal of each part is to fulfill some aspect of them reaching *their* goal. All we have to do is choose the stories and lessons from your life that align with your goals. From there, we just talk it out and edit. Sound like a plan?"

He leaned back and nodded his head. "Well, yeah. When you put it like that, it sounds easy."

If it sounds easy to you, that's because it is, once you understand how a book is built. What I'd like to do in this chapter is give you a brief overview of the shape of a book so that you can understand how to build your own. This is probably what *most* of you came for, so I'll try to be as clear as possible here.

THE SHAPE OF A BOOK

There are lots of ways that books can take shape, but the easiest way to think about it is to break it up into three primary sections. You can think of your book as having an intro (not to be confused with the "Introduction"), a body, and a conclusion (not to be confused with the "Conclusion"). Even if your book has multiple parts or has no formal introduction or conclusion, you can still follow this elementary formula.

Think back to writing an essay. You had these exact same sections, and in each section you had a different goal. The intro paragraph was all about orienting your reader to your topic by providing context and introducing your thesis statement (topic sentence). The body paragraphs were there to make your case, whether you were arguing a point or simply informing. The conclusion was the wrap-up, where you summarized your main ideas and offered your closing statements. (In more sophisticated papers, these remarks are often a look at the implications of the material in a broader sense, even looking toward the future.)

Believe it or not, this works just as well for a book—it just looks a little different. Consider this rudimentary outline:

Introduction
o I am going to teach you how to write a book in thirty days

Body
o Step 1: Clarify your "why"
o Step 2: Clear your calendar
o Step 3: Define your reader
…
o Step 7: Edit and revise

Conclusion
o I have shown you how to write a book quickly and efficiently

If you break down this book (yes, the one you're reading), it fits into this outline perfectly. But as I said, it looks a little different. This is because you can structure these sections however you like, as long as you achieve the goals. For a book, the goals of each section are a little more expansive than in your standard essay, but they can be summarized as follows:

Introduction
o Define the purpose for the book (Explain the problem the book solves & describe the outcome)
o Identify who the book is for
o Introduce the author (Primarily their credibility)
o Orient reader to what's ahead and how to read the book

Body
o Clarify misconceptions about the problem (Provide the true solution)
o Offer conceptual knowledge about the topic
o Provide practical knowledge about the topic
o Give readers actionable steps

Conclusion
o Address objections
o Summarize main ideas
o Provide positive outlook for the future (Leave readers on positive emotions)
o Invite readers to other products or services.

This outline is a more comprehensive look at the goals of each section. If you accomplish each of these goals, your book will be simple, clear, practical, and useful. It follows a flow of thought that we are trained through school to understand and that has been optimized for didactic purposes.

Imagine picking up a book that started with chapter 1 and offered no context around what you're supposed to be learning. You'd be a little lost, right? You'd probably ask questions like, "What is this?" and "Why do I care?" That is how your reader would feel without any sort of introductory section. Another way to think about this beginning portion of your book is as your official handshake. You're making first contact and showing readers that you can be trusted.

It's obvious that, without the body, there is simply no book. What's important and often overlooked is how you deliver your content. If you don't teach readers the concepts *and* provide actionable steps (let's say you do one or the other), you risk giving them unusable information or directions they don't understand. Like a bad recipe. Both elements are necessary to make your material stick.

Finally, without the conclusion, you leave your readers swimming in uncontextualized information with no direction on what to do with it. Moreover, you miss an opportunity to make a strong lasting impression on your readers that solidifies you in their minds. Without that, the question arises, "What was the point of writing your book?" I want to give you just one more outline, detailing one way your book may come together given what I've just shared:

Introduction
Preface
o How this book came to be
o What inspired it

Introduction
o Why this book
o Who it's for
o Who are you
o How to read this book

Body
Chapter 1 – Step 1 in solving problem
Chapter 2 – Step 2 in solving problem
…
Chapter 10 – Step 10 in solving problem

Conclusion
Conclusion
o Address objections
o Summarize main ideas
o Provide positive outlook for the future
o Invite readers to other products or services

Hopefully now you're starting to see the shape of your book fairly clearly. I understand this is just a framework, so the next two sections touch more on what goes into each of them.

THE INTRO AND CONCLUSION

Take a moment and think about the last book you read. Where did you start reading? Did you read the preface and introduction? If there was a foreword, did you read that? If you're like most readers, probably not.

Many readers, especially if they are short on time, will look for the first point of content that they feel is relevant to them. Often, this means skipping "front matter" and going straight to chapter 1. Front matter is the material *before* the main content of a book. It typically includes the title page, copyright page, table of contents, epigraph, foreword, and preface. The introduction is technically a part of the main content, but it often gets lumped in with front matter. (Note: readers still expect some context or setup. They just assume what's in the introduction is just "extra" setup.)

If you look at the last outline I provided, you'll see that the preface and introduction contain a lot of setup and relationship-building between the author and the reader. Essentially, those parts have all of the material designed to show the book's value to your reader and start creating a connection with you, the author. You can't really afford for readers to skip that.

This is why I generally teach my premium clients to shift all of that information into the first two or three chapters. If you want to pace your book out, or potentially need to add more content because your main content is short, I recommend three. If you have a lot of core content or an impatient audience, then I recommend just two.

In this book, I've included a preface, but I still put all of the important information into the first three chapters. To me, it was worth it to take the time and use that space to build a connection with readers. (Hopefully it worked!) So this book and my first, *Facing Racism*, are perfect examples of this strategy. In short, it looks like this: chapter 1 defines the book's problem and purpose to show the reader you understand them. Chapter 2 highlights a segment of your personal story with the problem to showcase your expertise and why you care. Chapter 3 introduces the core concepts and provides a road map to the rest of the book.

Done this way, these chapters can be very short—a few pages at most, usually. The other method, using two chapters, combines chapters 1 and 2 from the approach above into one. In practice, this works by dividing the chapter into subsections. (Using subheadings is optional, but effective for expedient reading.) Then chapter 2 is about setting the stage for the rest of the book. An outline of the first chapters may look like this if you use just two:

Chapter 1: So You Want to Write a Book?
o I Get It, Writing a Book is Hard
o How I Got Into Writing and Editing

Chapter 2: The Book Builder Method
o Why Is Now the Best Time to Write?
o What Is the Method?
o How to Read This Book

Do you see how using this strategy shifts the relationship-building information into the main content? In choosing to break with tradition, you are actually extending your handshake and maintaining contact with your reader. You are slowly getting their buy-in. Even before you start to teach the reader, they are unconsciously starting to like and believe in you through the personality you share in these stories. (As a note on form, each point listed beneath the chapter title can be used to represent its own subsection.)

Next, I want to talk about the conclusion section. (I'll come back to the content in just a moment because there is a lot to unpack there, and I want to give it adequate space.) In the conclusion, remember that you have four goals: address objections, summarize main ideas, provide a positive outlook for the future, and invite readers to other products or services.

You can accomplish this in one chapter using subheadings, and it would be perfectly acceptable. Another option is to break this up into two smaller chapters: one for objections and obstacles and another for summarizing and looking ahead.

I am personally a fan of the latter method because the material feels less like a long wrap-up and more like regular content. This means the reader stays engaged just a little longer, and you have the opportunity to add more value for them. I think the easiest way to explain this would be to show you.

In *Facing Racism*, I understood that my readers might struggle heavily with some of the topics I covered in the main body. To combat this, I dedicated an entire chapter just to helping them overcome some of the challenges that they would face. In the images below, you will see snippets from that chapter to get an idea of what this looks like in practice:

12

NOT AN EASY ROAD

"Success is not final, failure is not fatal, it is the courage to continue that counts."

— WINSTON CHURCHILL

Unlearning generations of white privilege and subconscious racial bias is not going to be easy or immediate. It's immensely personal, difficult, and existential work that may make you feel things you don't fully understand. You might become embarrassed. You might feel anger toward other white people who aren't putting themselves through the same intense work. You might even question more than just your thoughts about race. You see, shadow work challenges you to question everything you previously took as secure, and exposing unconscious racial bias may make you question if you really are a good person like you thought. (How could you be if you never saw these things, right?)

But because of this intense work, committing to this process will do more for you as a person than eliminate racism. It will radically transform your way of thinking by opening your mind to things you couldn't see before. It's the work that will allow you to "check your privilege" and walk a mile in the other guy's shoes. It'll empower you to take control over your thoughts and notice

Sample Reading 1 from Facing Racism *(2020)*

What I've done in the example on the previous page is create space for my readers to mess up without feeling ashamed. I've given them an honest glimpse at what will come up for them that hasn't been mentioned in previous chapters.

Doing this allowed me to build a stronger relationship with them because it looks like I really took the time to think about them as people and understand their need for support. These are pitfalls they could not have foreseen, and instead of leaving my readers to encounter them alone, I prepared them.

Throughout the chapter, I utilized subheadings to introduce a new potential pitfall and devoted a few paragraphs to addressing them. (See the following images.)

> NO. 2 – RESISTANCE
>
> Previously, we talked about facing resistance from others during courageous conversations. What stops people from succeeding with these steps, though, is not resistance from others but from themselves. When confronted with questions that challenge your integrity, your first reaction is to reject it. It is a natural self-preservation tactic that the ego employs because it is built of all the beliefs you've accumulated to this point. What this leads to is an innate resistance to the discoveries.

Sample Reading 3 from Facing Racism *(2020)*

> NO. 3 – NOT ENOUGH PATIENCE
>
> Because this is such intense work, it's going to take time to implement and get used to practicing. The "purification of the soul" is a life-long process of refinement. There is no point at which you're "done." You just get progressively better as you continue the work.
>
> Where so many people lose traction is that they feel like it's taking too long. I remember when I helped my friend get over a bad breakup. Her ex had been cheating on her and she didn't find out until he finally left for the other woman. She was so torn at first, but over time she started to heal. One day, she asked me about my last break up and if I still thought about my ex.

Sample Reading 4 from Facing Racism *(2020)*

As you can see, there is actually quite a bit to talk about in an objections or obstacles chapter. For brevity, I've only shared small fragments. Still, I hope you're seeing the potential of a chapter like this. Choosing not to include one not only costs you a chance to make a really good impression, but also a chance to address any objections your reader may have.

Think about it! Throughout your book, your reader will be imagining all the reasons your method wouldn't work for them. You have space in this chapter to show them why these reasons are valid but actually irrelevant.

This is a perfect place to include real-life case studies and testimonials—without being overtly sales-y. This is also where I advise most authors to place an invitation to work together. That usually takes the form of, "Now, I've given you all of the tools to overcome your own hurdles, but I recognize that your circumstances may be unique and you may want more help adapting this method to your life. If that is the case, on the Thank You page I've included a way to contact me directly so we can talk about your situation and develop a plan that works for you." (Hint hint.)

This creates a perfect segue into the conclusion chapter. The conclusion is not complicated. In essence, you'll simply want to recap any core concepts so that they stick in your readers' minds. Then offer readers some encouragement for their journey ahead. The important thing here is that your readers *feel* like they've gotten everything, like you didn't hold anything back, and that you are on their side. (Because you are!)

The conclusion is *not* a place to sell. Your book should do all of the selling for you by addressing their problem and showing your value as an expert. Here, you want to show your value as their ally or partner. This is the space for you to let go of your ego and lean into empathy as a human being. Show compassion and understanding. It's all about building a likable persona. You want your readers to know that you've got their backs and you're here to help, not to sell them an expensive package. You've already extended an invite in the objections chapter, so you don't need to reiterate it here. A book is about giving, and the best way to give is to avoid attaching an ask to it.

THE CORE CONTENT

I know we've covered a lot in this chapter, but this is perhaps the second-most-important chapter in the book. Most people fail to write their books because they have no idea how to structure them, let alone put them together in a way that is *designed* to make an impact and win the buy-in of their readers. Now you are a part of the small percentage of people who do.

Of course, this chapter would not be complete if we didn't talk about how to choose and organize your content. This is something I hear so many aspiring authors struggle with. They have all these ideas and have no clue how to organize them. They don't know what to put in the book, what to leave out, or what order to put it in.

Unfortunately, many people either give up there or spend hours researching "how to write a book," downloading free e-books, and signing up for free workshops that don't teach anything unless they buy the full program. This is not what I'm doing here. (You can relax.) Below, I've included *two* easy methods I teach to my clients and writing students to help them get their ideas onto the page.

Before I dive in, though, do you remember what I said about your ideal reader being the key to your whole book? This is where the reader and the topic have a big impact on your writing process. The simplest way to put it is that your reader decides the content. Everything you include will be chosen with one goal in mind: to help your ideal reader (not everyone possible, but your true ideal reader) to solve their one specific problem. Remember, your reader doesn't need to know everything about finances in order to fix their credit.

When I was planning this book, there were a number of things I wanted to include that just didn't fit into the scope of this project. Things like creating front and back matter, building your launch team, planning your launch, marketing after launch, applying for speaking gigs—all of these are great talking points, but I had to remember why you came to *this* book in particular.

You are a successful entrepreneur, so I can assume you have some grasp of marketing. You may want to do more speaking gigs, but right now you want to know how to write your book. So that is what I've promised to give you. Anything else would get filed away as extra in your mind, and when you're ready for that material, you'll likely go buy a more complete and focused book. So why not make this one hyper-focused?

So, with that in mind, how do you come up with your content? I suggest one of the two following methods.

Method 1 – The Road Map

The first method is more comprehensive, but it works every time. I call it the road map method because you basically create a detailed road map of your book. Here are the steps (keep in mind that it can be helpful to use a spreadsheet rather than a piece of paper):

1. Brain Dump. Make a list of all the things you want to teach or talk about. This may be anywhere from fifty to 200 items. Just write them down. Don't worry about the order. At this point, you just want to see what is in your head.

2. Categorize. Take similar and related items and put them together by theme. If you have ten points about what your reader should expect when they go to the bank, you can group those ten in a "going to the bank" category. Do this until you have between six and twelve categories. These categories will make up your middle chapters.

3. Purpose. Write a clear purpose statement for each category based on the theme or point you want to make for your reader. Your purpose statement is the key to that chapter. It should be one clear sentence highlighting your intent for your reader. This is more than the chapter's topic. Think in terms of outcome. How will your reader be different at the end of the chapter? What will they have learned? What will they be able to do? As an example, my purpose statement for this chapter was, "My reader will learn how to choose and organize their content, as well as how to structure their book."

4. Organize. This is the tricky part. Arrange the chapters in a way that makes sense. There should be an orderly flow from one topic to the next, with topics building on each other. Start with easier ideas and move into harder ones. Think about where your reader is and where you want them to be. For example, in *Facing Racism*, it was clear that my readers didn't understand enough history to be able to talk about modern events in a racial context. In addition to that, they were *really* uncomfortable with talking about race. So the first chapters are all about getting comfortable with the material and looking at the big picture without feeling triggered. Only after that would they feel comfortable enough to address more complex ideas around race, prejudice, and bias.

5. Outline. Once you have all of your chapters, make a small outline for each one. Think about stories you want to include. You don't have to go into extreme detail about which idea to talk about first. That is where some people get stuck. The important thing is that you don't go into the chapter blind.

This method is for the people who need a full picture. This is for the planners who need to see where they're going every step of the way. This is also the recommended path for the person who tends to get lost without a plan. The purpose of this method is to figure out so much detail about your book before you write that, when the time comes, you know exactly what you want to say, even if it's not perfect. (We'll talk about perfectionism later.)

Method 2 – The Compass

The second method is simpler, but it tends to work best for people who really, really know what they're talking about. It's called the "compass" method because it gives the writer direction without any detail. These people typically have a fully fleshed-out course, or they teach their content so regularly that they only need a few bullet points to know what they're talking about. Here are those steps:

1. List Your Steps. List all the steps to solving your ideal reader's problem in the way that you would go through them in your program. If you only have four or five core steps, I recommend looking to see which ones contain sub-steps so you can break them into two chapters.

2. Purpose. Create a purpose statement for each step like I explained in the Road Map Method.

3. Talking Points. Give yourself three to five talking points per step. Instead of a detailed outline, you're just looking for a few points that you know you talk about over and over and that are essential to your teaching.

4. Organize. Make sure your steps are in an order that your ideal reader can follow easily in a book. The guidance in the previous method applies here too.

If you choose this method, you can jump straight into writing. The main caveat is that you have less insurance against writer's block. This method is for the intuitive person who sucks at planning but always gets done if they have enough time and enough room.

No matter which method you choose, the important takeaway from this section is that you choose a framework for uncovering your content. Once you do, you will have the blueprint to writing your book. The more detail you add at this phase, the more clarity you will have when you sit down to write. Remember that clear writing is often a product of clear thinking. A little forethought can go a long way.

ACTIVITY

This chapter is all about planning your content and bringing structure to your book. In this activity, you're going to take what you've learned so far and put it together to develop a high-level overview of your book's framework.

For your first step, decide on the book structure you want to use. Would you prefer a traditional preface, introduction, and conclusion? Or would you prefer to insert that material into the main content of your book? If you decide to use chapters, how many will you use? Once you've decided, you want to commit to that structure. Open a new document in your word processor and type the following:

(Modify this according to your choice.)

INTRODUCTION
Chapter 1: [Working Title]
Purpose: At the end of this chapter, my reader will… [insert result].
Chapter 2: [Working Title]
Purpose: At the end of this chapter, my reader will… [insert result].

BODY
[insert Body chapters]

CONCLUSION
Chapter Y: [Working Title]
Purpose: At the end of this chapter, my reader will… [insert result].
Chapter Z: [Working Title]
Purpose: At the end of this chapter, my reader will… [insert result].

Next, decide which strategy you would like to use to develop your body content. If you have a lot of pre-created content, then the Compass Method should be sufficient. If you want a more detailed plan, use the Road Map Method. If you are going the Compass route, open a new document in your word processor and type out all of the steps of your program. Follow the steps above to develop an initial outline of your content.

Once you have the steps to your program (a.k.a. your process for taking the reader from where they are with the problem to the result) and they are organized in the best way you can conceive, insert them into your skeleton in the body section. Be sure to give each one an official chapter number and a working title. Below is my final chapter summary for this book as an example. I used the Compass Method:

INTRODUCTION
Preface – How this Book Came to Be
Chapter 1 – The Problem with Books
Purpose: My reader will see that I understand his struggle to write a book while running his business.
Chapter 2 – Who am I
Purpose: My reader will get to know my experience with writing a book in a crunch.
Chapter 3 – Book Proposals + How to Read This Book

Purpose: My reader will get a little insight into the bookmaking process as well as a roadmap to how to read and use this book

BODY

Chapter 4 – What is a Book + Goals
Purpose: My reader will get a working understanding of how a book differs from other lead magnets, why people write and read books, how a book can help them and their specific goals for their book.

Chapter 5 – Create Space + Commitment
Purpose: My reader will understand that no matter how busy they are, they will have to create space and commit to the work. This is true for every goal.

Chapter 6 – Define Your Reader
Purpose: My reader will learn why it is important to define the reader early, how the reader shapes the book, and how to get super clear on their ideal reader.

Chapter 7 – Define Your Topic
Purpose: My reader will learn to clearly define the problem their book solves for their reader and how this serves as the core of the book's topic.

Chapter 8 – Content & Structure
Purpose: My reader will learn how to choose and organize their content, as well as how to structure their book

Chapter 9 – Ready to Write (Writing Pace + Hacks)
Purpose: My reader will get clear about their writing process and some key strategies to make writing easy and efficient. They will develop their unique writing plan.

Chapter 10 – Writing the First Draft
Purpose: My reader will get a clear picture of what to and not to do when writing their first draft. They will see how executing their specific plan leads to easy success.

Chapter 11 – Editing Secrets
Purpose: My reader will learn the comprehensive editing process,

essentials for self-editing, and how to seek a professional for assistance.

Chapter 12 – Title, Description, Cover
Purpose: My reader will learn the secret to choosing a good title, how to write an enticing description that sells, and how to design their cover (or choose a designer)

CONCLUSION

Chapter 13 – Writer's block or Writing Blocks
Purpose: My reader will understand what writer's block really is, where it comes from and how to get out of it.

Chapter 14 – Conclusion
Purpose: My reader feel hopeful about their role as a bourgeoning author.

Appendix 1 – Front matter/Back matter

As one final note for this chapter, you should know that the preface and appendix are what is considered front matter and back matter. I've explained these in the official Appendix of the book.

9

READY TO WRITE

1. Working Title ____
2. Hook or Tagline ⭐
3. Book Description ____
4. Target Market ⭐
5. Market Analysis (why your book is relevant) ⭐
6. Marketing Plan ____
7. Author Bio ____
8. Chapter Summary ⭐
9. Production Details (length, format, completion date, etc.) ____
10. Sample Chapter ____

Completed Elements in a formal Book Proposal 1

If you have done all of the activities, you should have what looks like the beginnings of a book proposal. Do you notice how some the items on the list have stars next to them? Those stars mean you have already created this material or at least had an opportunity to think about it. In the coming chapters, we'll talk more about your description, author bio, and title. In this chapter, we're going to develop your production details and get you "ready to write."

Technically speaking, you *do not* need every element on this list to actually write your manuscript. I am providing it to you so you can see just how far you've already come. After this chapter, you will be perfectly equipped to write, at least in terms of preparation. The final piece of this "prepare to write" puzzle is your writing plan, which ensures you can take action once you have your book blueprint.

FIND YOUR FLOW

In chapter 5, I gave you some tips on how to open space and fit book work into your calendar. To this point all of your "book work" has been planning. Now it's time to get down to writing. I mentioned before that, in general, it may take about thirty hours to write a chapter. That is a great baseline number to shoot for, but in order for you to be the most successful, we want to determine *your* writing pace.

When I work with authors in my program, before they begin writing, I urge them to find what I call their "author flow state." In short, this is a state of writing when words and ideas are flowing effortlessly and they are creating, uninhibited by doubts, fear, and confusion. In this state, you essentially lose track of time because you are tuned in to your message and allowing whatever comes in to flow out. Let me give you a non-book example that may help you understand this concept.

When I was in college at Arizona State, I didn't have the luxury of a car, so I rode my bike everywhere. Whether it was from class to class or to the grocery store or out for a workout, you would probably see me whizzing by on my navy-blue Schwinn hybrid.

One day, I went out for a workout, determined to ride

fifteen miles (which isn't much to any *serious* cyclist but was a legitimate goal for me at the time). I put a bottle of ice water in the bottle holder, tucked my sweat towel into my waistband, and headed out. The first few miles were easy because my muscles were just warming up, and I hadn't gotten into the real workout. At about mile four, I started to feel my breath getting heavier and the strain on my muscles.

By mile five, I was thoroughly uncomfortable. *Come on, Drae. We just getting started!* I thought. *This is easy stuff.* I needed to go at least two more miles before I could turn around. That would bring my round-trip ride to my goal of fifteen miles. So I kept pedaling and tried to modulate my breathing, taking small sips of water as needed.

I can't say exactly when it happened, mile six or mile seven, but before long, my breathing, pedaling, and sips were in sync, and it felt like my body switched to autopilot. The fatigue disappeared from my mind, along with almost everything else that wasn't my breath or the music in my ears. I was in a zone, following the street and bike trails to who knows where. It didn't really matter; all that mattered was that I didn't even think about stopping.

Eventually, I did stop. The sky was starting to change from orange to pink, with deep blue encroaching where the sun's rays no longer reached. It was getting late and I had *no idea* where I was. I took note of the nearest building—some Asian restaurant in a small plaza—and turned back to ride home. At that time I didn't have a smart phone, so I couldn't just look up my way back on GPS. I would have to navigate back with just my eyes and look up where I had gone from my computer when I got back to the dorms.

The ride back was longer than expected. How far had I gone? I arrived at my dorm just after sunset. I was tired, but eager to figure out if I had reached my goal. I pulled out my computer and searched the restaurant on Google Maps. The directions made sense, but something was wrong. The directions said that the restaurant was twelve miles away. If that were true, I would have ridden a total of twenty-four miles! I had been in a flow state.

When you're "in flow," you aren't thinking; you're feeling. You tap into the part of yourself that knows what you need to say, and you allow yourself to write. This state is automatic and is very likely the time when you will type the fastest in your writing process. While we can't force our way into flow state, we can imagine what it would be like to be there. To do this, I encourage my authors to try a short exercise.

Choose a time and go to your writing place. Open your word processor to a blank document. Set a timer for thirty minutes and write on one of the following three prompts:

1. What is the most important secret that your reader needs to know to solve their problem?
2. Who are you and how did you come to solve the problem? What experience do you have?
3. What is your wish for the reader?

Type for the full thirty minutes without stopping. If you feel yourself getting stuck, just keep typing your random thoughts until you pick back up somewhere. If you run out of ideas for the prompt you have chosen, skip a line and pick up again writing about another prompt. (It may help to choose your backup before you start, just in case.) Once the timer goes off, stop writing—even if your sentence is not finished.

Record the number of words you have written. In Microsoft Word, it will be visible somewhere near the bottom of the page. In Google Docs, you can turn this on by selecting "Tools" and then "Word Count" from the top of the screen. This number will be the total words you would type in half an hour. So to get your words per hour, you would simply double this number. If your total words written in thirty minutes is 500, then your words per hour in your flow state is 1,000 words per hour. (For most people it's higher than this, but I'm using simple numbers to illustrate the point here.)

This number will help you determine exactly how much time you will need in order to write your book. If the average chapter length for books in your genre is 2,500 words and you write 1,000 words per hour, you would need two and a half hours to write that chapter. That's a total of thirty-seven and one-half hours for a fifteen-chapter book. Although you'll probably need a little more.

The higher your flow state pace, the faster your book can be written. The good news is that, by creating the plan earlier, you've given yourself all the information you need to stay more inspired while writing. (Meaning shorter writing times!)

HOW YOU WRITE

This brings me to another important point. Do you remember how I mentioned earlier that we speak more words per minute than we type? Well, what this means is that, if you can utilize dictation or transcription, then you can radically increase the pace at which you write your book. For example, when my dad and I set out to actually write his book together, we had meetings on Zoom.

He and I had created a very detailed plan using the Road Map Method. Because he is not a writer, we determined it would be easiest if he just told me his stories and delivered his message as if we were having a conversation. I recorded the Zoom meetings with him talking and then I imported the audio into a transcription software. The software I use is Otter.ai. There are many other services out there that do a great job. This is just the one that I used because I had heard good reviews about it.

By transcribing his book, my dad was able to tell his stories comfortably and naturally. This allowed him to get into his personal flow state and dramatically increase his word count per chapter in a short amount of time. In a thirty-minute span, we were able to capture nearly 3,000 words per chapter. Of course, not all of them were usable. When we speak, there are often mini filler words that take up space and have to be deleted during the editing phase. Even so, that does not negate the fact that he wrote and finished an initial draft of every chapter in just a few writing sessions.

We usually met for an hour to an hour and a half, depending on how much time was available to both of us, and we were able to record at least two chapters per session. If you are tech-savvy and like to optimize your productivity, dictation is a good way to enhance your workflow by capitalizing on the benefits of natural speech versus written text. As one more piece of evidence, about 50 percent of this book was initially created through dictation using a combination of Apple's speech-to-text software and Otter.ai. Dictation was a part of *my* writing success plan.

(Note: Dictation is an imperfect science. You can expect a few more errors as the software interprets what you say. So try to speak clearly and deliberately.)

This is also the point when many non-writers consider hiring a ghostwriter. There is this idea that if you pay someone to write your book for you, you can save a lot of time and it'll come out better. This is why we hire experts for a lot of different things; they know what they're doing and can often do it better than we can as novices. What I want you to know, though, is that ghostwriting can still be a time commitment because you have to meet with your writer to conduct interviews and review their work for approval.

You are also beholden to their workflow and writing pace. If you want your book done in three months or less, but the fastest they can do it is in six, you will be stuck with their pace. Most ghostwriters will not expedite the process just because you want them to. On top of that, ghostwriting can be a very costly option, and one you may not be fully prepared to invest in. I am not against ghostwriting. I just think that, while talking about different ways to write your book, it is important to mention some of the details around that particular method. If you don't have a tight deadline and you do have a big budget for your book, then hiring a ghostwriter can ease a lot of pressure and allow you to still operate in your business. Done-for-you service is a great way to maximize your productivity by leveraging your resources. It allows you to stay in your zone of genius, work in your business, and know that progress is being made on your book. The most important factor is making sure that you are partnered with someone who you trust and who truly understands you, your voice, your message, and your goals.

YOUR UNIQUE SUCCESS PLAN

Suppose you discovered one hour a day available on your calendar and chose to block it out for book work. Now you get to assess that time block against how much time you actually need in order to write one chapter in your book. If you write 2,000 words per hour, you can finish the chapter in one hour because the minimum word count for each chapter is about 1,500. If you set yourself a target of one chapter per hour, then you can have your book done in about fifteen hours, give or take.

What you must do now is revisit the time block that you've chosen to make sure it still feels like the most creative and productive time of day for you as well as the best time available in your schedule to write. The difference between what you are doing now versus what you did in chapter 5 is that in this chapter you want to focus not only on when you're available to work on your book but when you're most productive. Are you more comfortable writing first thing in the morning or at night after you eat and everyone else in your household has gone to bed? Do you have children and responsibilities that distract you during normal hours?

I want you to be able to eliminate as many distractions as possible during your chosen time. The less there is to pull your mind away from your writing, the more successful you can be. This brings me to another crucial point, which is to control your environment. This means your internal environment, such as your mindset, your emotions, your health, and your energy at the times that you've chosen to write. This also means your external environment. Where do you choose to write?

I love to write in different places. While I do have my home office set up, I find that I can only stay at that one place for so long and maintain my focus. It helps me to have a few different places to write, such as the front porch, the local coffee shop, the university library, and, on occasion, my bed. All of these spaces are ideal for me because they support my comfort as well as my focus on the task at hand. If I start getting uncomfortable at my desk, I shift to my bed. If I'm uncomfortable in the house, I go outside, or I go to a coffee shop or library.

You may not be like me. You may need to write in the same place every time like one of my former mentees, who designated a specific desk in her home as the place where she would do all of her writing work. At her desk, she built a small altar and placed little reminders, supportive notes, and images designed to draw out her creativity and encourage her when she felt uninspired. She also kept a few of her favorite books as inspiration, so whenever she needed a quick boost or to get back in touch with her inner writer, she would open one of them and read a small passage.

Do you have anything like that, a book or some totem to

help you get into your writing flow and build your creative energy? What sort of rituals do you have that you can include before, during, or after you write? For example, every time I prepared to write this book, I liked to read one short paragraph from my previous book to help me get in touch with my voice. Then I would meditate for about five minutes, to ensure clarity in my mind. While I'm writing, I try not to work for any longer than thirty minutes at a time, unless I'm really in a flow. Instead, I stand up, stretch, and do little movements to keep blood flowing through my body.

To end each writing session, it was helpful, or at least encouraging, to thank myself for the focused time. This may sound strange at first, but for me it was a small acknowledgment that the writing session was successful, however it was. It can be really easy to get discouraged if you don't feel like you ever get into a flow state. That is perfectly okay. By expressing gratitude toward yourself after the writing session, you allow yourself to feel good about your accomplishment, which supports your desire to come back and do it again in the next session.

Putting all this together, you'll be able to create your own unique writing plan. This plan will include when you write, where you write, and how long you write for. Based on this, you can give yourself a clear deadline. For some, deadlines sound scary. This is because they are a commitment, and sometimes people can be afraid to truly commit. But you've already done that. Having a deadline reinforces what you already promised yourself.

By giving yourself a clear deadline, you hold yourself accountable to both the plan and a goal. Remember, people will take as much time as you give them. If someone has three months to write a book, they will take three months. If they have six weeks, they will take six weeks. By giving yourself a clear deadline, you hold yourself accountable to both the plan and a goal by making it time-bound.

This is how you can derive both your completion date and your book length. If you know each chapter is going to be roughly 2,000 words, and you've planned out fifteen chapters, then you can assume that your book will be roughly 30,000 words. Based on your specific plan to write those 30,000 words, you can choose a realistic completion date.

This is tied to the book's form as well because you've already built the outline for your book. You know exactly what structure you're going to put it in and how it will take shape. The only additional information you will need to know for finalization (which is a topic for another time, since this book is about how to finish your manuscript) is the size and thickness of the book.

In short, there are a few standard print sizes, the most common for nonfiction being 5 in. x 8 in. and 6 in. x 9 in. Page count is determined by word count as well as font size, line spacing, and margins, which are all factors that an interior designer will take care of for you. You could learn to format your own book, but it will take you much more time to learn the skills, and the result may not be as good as if you hired a professional from the start. I just included the basic information here so you have a general idea of what comes in production.

ACTIVITY

For this chapter's activity, you want to take some time to determine your peak writing pace in flow state and use that to create your unique writing success plan. Use the exercise from earlier, including the questions, to determine your flow state. Then review your calendar to make sure that the time that you've allotted for working on your book still matches when you were most productive.

Finally, analyze your space to determine if it is where you want to work on your book. If not, think of two or three places where you would rather go to write your book. Just make sure that they are accessible to you and that you can actually spend time there. Once you've done this, you will be able to begin writing.

10

WRITING YOUR FIRST DRAFT

Alright, I'll be honest with you: the first draft of any book is always the most intimidating. This is because, even after you've planned out the book and everything you intend to say, when faced with a blank page, people have a tendency to forget... everything! In this chapter, I want to spend a little time talking about how to effectively write your first draft from start to finish, as well as cover a few core writing topics that will make your book stand out.

One of the first things that you should know about writing your first draft is that it doesn't have to be perfect. Author Terry Pratchett once said, "The first draft is just you telling yourself the story." What he's getting at here is that, while writing the first draft, you don't really know where you're going or where you're going to end up. All you have is your road map to guide you, but often writers, when they get into their flow, deviate from the plan, and what they create is a little different from what they expected. Sometimes it's not great, but many times it's better.

Your core takeaway here is that you don't want to focus on getting things exactly right the first time. Nobody does that. In fact, in her book *Bird by Bird,* author Anne Lamott talks about what she calls the "shitty first draft," the certainty that your first draft will be your worst. That you're going to feel like it's no good and half the time you're unsure of what you're trying to say.

It's rare that any writer of any caliber can sit down and start typing their best work straight from their head. Even those who write eloquently still get have their work edited to ensure that their books are of the highest quality possible. And often, before they reach editing, which we will talk about later in the book, these authors will go through at least a couple more drafts.

In this process, it isn't necessary for you to go through multiple drafts of your book. You just need to get through one. Once you've gotten through your first draft, revising is easy, and you can bring on help. (Although taking the time to revise your work yourself can add a ton of value, ease the workload on your editorial team, and save you money.)

If there's nothing else that you come away with from this chapter, let it be that your first draft is between you and the blank page. Of course, you always want to be writing to your ideal reader, but know that they will never see your first draft or any of its imperfections. This is your opportunity to let loose and show up 100 percent. As a business owner and coach, you probably aren't very shy when it comes to working with your clients; however, writing a book is new territory and these feelings tend to come up. I understand that this is your space to be vulnerable and choose courage.

Brené Brown (I'm sure you've heard of her!) talks about vulnerability and how, without it, there is no courage. If you expect your book to create transformation in your readers, you have to be willing to go through transformation within yourself. The writing phase is where you discover yourself, your fears, your anxieties, your doubts. This is your opportunity to do the personal alchemy and live the growth you intend to replicate in your clients. This brings me to my second major point.

TELL STORIES

One of the number one ways for your reader to be able to connect with you as an authority in your industry as well as a person that they know, like, and trust is through reading your personal stories. As experts in our fields, it can be really easy to want to strictly teach. This is natural, if you think about it, because whenever we go to learn something we think of our time at school and how teachers just deliver the lessons. Only, they don't. At least, the best ones don't.

If you went to college, I want you to think back to your absolute least favorite professor. What did you dislike about them? Aside from probably assigning way more work than is necessary or reasonable for their class, chances are their teaching style really didn't resonate with you. Why do you think that is? If I had to guess, I would say that it's because all they did was read off the slides and talk at you. They probably weren't very engaging, except to ask questions to unsuspecting students in the last row.

I had a professor like this. That was one of my worst classes because I found it difficult to keep my focus on the lecture. That professor read off of slides and expected the class simply to take notes the entire time. Eventually, my mind would wander, and before I knew it, I had missed a handful of slides and their valuable content.

I remember one class session where I completely checked out. We were learning about *Beowulf*, a story I actually enjoy, but the way she "taught" was so insufferable that my mind ran off to all the other things I had to do that day: finish a paper for my sociology class, visit a restaurant for a writing assignment in ENG 102, email my advisor about getting into the French program… and something else…

"Andrae?"

I shook my head and looked up. Apparently, she had called on me to answer a question about the text. The class was waiting for my answer, and in that moment, so was I.

"I, um… Could you repeat the question?" I said.

"No. I'm sure one of your classmates has it." She called on another student, who gave a very academic answer—that is to say his answer was a pretentious and scholarly way of saying that he liked the book and agreed with the professor's take. (What a suck-up!)

This is a huge contrast with my *favorite* professor of the year: my sociology professor. He was a tall man with a long, dark ponytail and tattoos. If you saw him, you would have mistaken him for a stereotypical biker because he had this stern, too-cool-for-school vibe. That is, until he appeared on stage in the lecture hall.

Every lecture started with a story of something he had experienced or observed that week. Sometimes it related to our reading. Sometimes it was just to prime our brains and wake us up. His least favorite thing was feeling like he was talking to a room full of cardboard cutouts. "Come on, you guys are students," he would say. "Your heads are full of so much shit, I know you have something to say."

Aside from his powerful character, what made him my favorite professor was that I felt like I learned more in his class than anywhere else. This is because he taught us using allegory —story. For every concept we had to learn, he gave a real-world example from his own life that made it real to us. Instead of just talking about stereotypes, for example, he shared a story about how he was perceived at a grocery store by an older woman who assumed he was a callous biker guy. She had no idea he actually held a PhD in sociology and taught at the university. All she saw were his clothes and tattoos, and she assumed he was dangerous.

Keep in mind that I took his class in 2013 or 2014. It's been at least seven years, and I still remember it because I can relate to it. That is what your readers want. They want to relate to you. You cannot be afraid to tell your personal stories. You cannot hide behind your knowledge. You have to show up in your book or you will never make a lasting impression on your readers.

It's been said over and over that people will forget what you say, but they'll never forget how you make them feel. The most evocative experience that humans have is stories. This is why we have fiction—short stories, novels, movies, television, theatre. Through stories, we share not only events but experiences, and that is what connects you to your reader. If you look back through the chapters of this book, you'll see that I've peppered stories throughout most of the chapters to help anchor you to the information.

Most readers will agree that powerful storytelling is what inspires them to action. It grabs and holds their attention and helps them to really understand the concepts at a deeper level. As you're writing your first draft, you want to be thinking about stories that you can include about your life or your clients' lives that both illustrate your key points and create an emotional impact on your readers.

Now, this doesn't mean that every idea needs a story. In fact, too much story can cause the message to get lost in some types of books. You will want to weave your storytelling into your chapters wherever it will significantly increase the reader's understanding of your message.

The main reason that I've found people shy away from storytelling is that they don't know how to do it. To help you, my reader, I want to give you a very brief rundown. Within your chapters, you can think of your stories as interplay between what you're teaching, "what happened when...," and what you think about it.

The easiest way to think about it is as if you were having a conversation with a friend. If you and your friend are talking about something and you remember a story of something that happened to you that's also related to what you and your friend are discussing, how would you tell that story? Then you just have to talk about what the story means to you and to your reader.

The thing about storytelling is understanding the goal. It's always about providing context. Sometimes you will want to use the story to set the stage for your main idea. Other times, the main idea comes first and the story paints the picture. What makes a story good is its relative closeness to the message, its relatability to the reader, and the ease with which it can be read.

As some general guidance, here are a few things to keep in mind when choosing and writing your stories:

1. Only tell stories that are relevant to the point you want to make in the chapter. While it may be interesting to you that you and your husband went skiing in Vail last winter, your reader is always asking, "So what?" and "What's the point?"
2. Get to the point. If you have a longer story, try not to waste too much time with buildup. Start as close to the action as possible. Trust the context of your content to lead the reader into the story as much as possible.
3. Incorporate some dialogue to get the reader "in scene." One of the major advantages of story is the option for you to break away from narration and vary your voice. If you review the stories in this book, most have some dialogue.

4. Stop at critical moments. The natural inclination is to tell how the story ends. This is generally a good rule of thumb, but in short nonfiction, the value and impact are not at the end of the story. Therefore, the retelling should stop where the value stops. (Notice how my college story earlier stops when my professor moves on?)
5. Close out major stories. Think back to chapter 1. That whole chapter was told in story, and the story *framed* my content. In this mode of storytelling, you *do* want to end the story by showing the resolution. In this case, the story structure is: character has problem > we decide to work together > the result.
6. Choose details that highlight significant elements to your point. For example, in chapter 1, I could have cut the segment about talking with Mollie before meeting Erin. It's effectively nonessential—except that it provides context about me, my work, my audience, and Erin as a client.
7. If you're starting your chapter with a story, ask yourself what questions it creates that you can answer. If your story comes in the middle or latter portion of a chapter, ask what questions it answers.
8. Don't think every story has to be long. Some stories can be as short as a paragraph. In this case you can incorporate more stories sometimes.
9. Harkening back to point one on this list, always *show* or state the relevance of a story explicitly. This is how you connect ideas with the reader.
10. Do not be afraid to fictionalize some parts of your story. In order to protect the identity of some people, you may feel inclined to remove identifying details about them or the locations involved. There may also be times where you can't remember the exact quotes,

times, or locations. It's okay to do a little staging as long as most of the story is legitimate.

CONNECT THE DOTS

One thing that you authors often forget is that the readers know nothing. What often happens is that the author, as an expert, uses language that the reader wouldn't understand and shares concepts in a very broad sweeping sense. Your job as the author in the self-help genre is not only to share your knowledge, but make it accessible and usable to your readers. You can't just show them the way, you have to connect the dots and clear the path so that the readers can get maximum understanding.

I once did edits on a metaphysical book that was both a memoir and a how-to guide on awakening to your spiritual power. The author was someone who has had their spiritual gifts since they were a child and who'd dedicated years to studying spirituality and occultism in many different books and from many different teachers back before they became accessible at places like Barnes & Noble. By all rights, this person was a true expert in the metaphysical.

His goal was to tell his story and teach people how they could also awaken to their spiritual powers like he had. When I read this manuscript, the first thing I thought was, *Wow, this is some really deep stuff. I love it!* The thing is, I've studied some of this for a few years myself. (I'm certainly not an expert.) As I got further into the book, though, I noticed the author had a bad habit of under-explaining important ideas. He would say things like, "There's a lot of information on this already, so I won't talk about it in this book" and "I'll talk more about this later" without ever getting back to it.

About halfway through the manuscript, I felt like *I* wanted to put the book on the shelf and take a break. There was so much mental work I had to do to understand some of his ideas, such as check out reference links and do Google searches for alternate meanings of words. I simply was not going to do that. And if I wasn't going to do it, his readers most certainly weren't either. If anyone did leave his book halfway through to check out one of those other books "out there," then they probably wouldn't remember enough about this guy to come back to his.

I asked him who his intended audience was.

"Spiritual babies," he said when we chatted.

I raised my eyebrow.

"I mean people who are brand-new to studying spirituality but always felt like they were different."

"Got it," I said. "Well, I can say that if you're writing to a total spiritual noob, you're speaking at too high a level. I'm 100 percent certain that the average newcomer is not going to know what half of this means, and if they go do outside research, they probably won't come back."

"Do you think I should write to a more mature crowd, then?"

"I think you already have. You have to decide who you most want to serve with this book, whether it's the newbie or the more experienced spiritualist. That will determine how much you need to explain and how much you can leave for them to know. The newbie reader has no experience, so if you've included something in the book, you have to break it down for them in ways that are simple. If they are more experienced, you can get away with scratching the surface. But that begs the question, what do you want to teach the more experienced reader?"

This calls back to what I mentioned previously about the ideal reader controlling the content. When you write to your ideal reader, you must use language that they would understand. If there is specific jargon that they need to know, you should take the time to explain it to them. You can define it in-text, with footnotes, or with a glossary of terms at the end of your book.

Remember that the reader is on a journey, and you are their tour guide. How you lead is how they will remember their experience and, ultimately, how they remember you.

(As a sidenote, this segment is an example of storytelling and connecting the dots.)

BUILD CHAPTERS BEFORE YOU WRITE

If you can't tell by now, I like planning. The more you know in advance, the easier it is to move forward with clarity. One area that I find many new authors struggle with is structuring their chapters. This is often because they don't take the time to organize their thoughts before they actually start writing.

When I wrote *Facing Racism*, I initially used the Compass Method. I was so eager to start writing. Planning out my content chapter by chapter felt like a chore and a waste of time. As an experienced writer and editor, I "knew" I would be able to move forward without that step.

When it came time to write, I started chapter 1 by simply telling a story. It was fresh in my mind from a conversation I had had not long prior, so writing it was easy. Chapter 2 told my story, and chapter 3 laid out the framework for the rest of the book. These chapters took no time to draft on the page.

At chapter 4, I felt my brain starting to stretch as I realized I wasn't sure what to say or where to start. Did I need to tell a story or teach a concept? How was I going to organize my thoughts for maximum flow? I ended up doing taking five minutes to create a rough outline for the chapter.

Just like with the three-part book outline we discussed in chapter 8 of this book, the outline for my chapter was composed of an introduction, body, and conclusion. The goals were pretty much the same as well: engage the reader, orient them to the topic, teach them my material, recap, and give final thoughts. Once I had that on paper, I wrote in what I needed to include to meet each goal. Ultimately, it looked something like this:

Intro
o Engage the reader – Story of Allison Cont.
o Define topic – Misconceptions about racism

Body
o Point 1 – Racism is not new or "coming back"
Example – learning history story
Reflect – it's an ongoing story
o Point 2 – White people don't have to feel guilty for the past
Example – BLM resistance
Reflect – You create the future now

Conclusion
o Core takeaways – We have to change together, now.
o Action item – Meditation

This basic outline took me five minutes to draft, but it brought me an abundance of clarity on how I wanted to write that chapter. This is the method I use now every time I have to write a document longer than a page. Here's how it works:

1. Review the chapter purpose to tune into your ideal reader's needs.
2. Create a blank outline using the three-part structure.
3. Assign subgoals to different parts of the chapter.
4. Assign specific stories and talking points to each goal.

Once you understand the way a chapter works—or rather, decide on how you want to organize your thoughts within the chapter—writing becomes easy. To be clear, the magic isn't explicitly in having a detailed outline, but in having taken five minutes to calm the nerves and bring focus to your thoughts.

And, just as a brief look, I would like to show you a revision of this outline if you were to write your chapter with a framing story:

Intro
o Engage the reader – Opening of story about Allison
o Inciting point – Direct attention to an observation or curiosity
o Define topic – Misconceptions about racism

Body
o Point 1 – Racism is not new or "coming back"
Example – Learning history story
Reflect – It's an ongoing story
Point back to story – What Alison didn't realize was...
o Point 2 – White people don't have to feel guilty for the past
Example – BLM resistance
Reflect – You create the future now

Conclusion
o Core takeaways – We have to change together, now.
o Resolve story – We talked, and the conversation with Allison inspired the content of this book...
o Action item – Meditation

At first glance, this may be hard to understand. What I've done is break down how the story I opened my other book with fits in across the scope of that chapter. In the intro, I set the stage and made the readers aware of a larger conversation that was coming. In the body, I pointed back to the story as I reflected on the content and examples. In the conclusion, I was sure to resolve the action of the scene by alluding to the end of a conversation that opened up more discussion (the rest of the book).

I could spend a whole chapter talking about the workings of a chapter, but I honestly think the detailed look into the form and inner workings of a chapter would be superfluous. You don't need to know how it works in order to write one. I've found the easiest way to write your chapter is to organize your thoughts and then "have a conversation" with your ideal reader.

Picture yourself in the conversation with them. They've asked you a question, and you've devoted this whole chapter to giving them the answer. An outline can be a great tool, but do not become reliant on it. Your goal is not simply to teach, but to connect.

USE YOUR OWN VOICE

Many authors think that they need to sound more esteemed or educated in order to write a good book. This couldn't be further from the truth. To be honest, the most impactful books in the genre actually feel conversational. Here are a few examples:

- *The 21 Irrefutable Laws of Leadership* (John C. Maxwell)
- *Daring Greatly* (Brené Brown)
- *Rich Dad Poor Dad* (Robert T. Kiyosaki)
- *Traffic Secrets* (Russell Brunson)

What you'll see in each of these is that the authors use a conversational tone that feels a lot like a conversation with a friend. To an extent, the writing been polished for publication, but it still feels friendly and inviting. These books have sold thousands of copies and are still impacting lives today.

This is because the authors don't try to be anything other than who they are. The key to a great book is not lofty language. It's an impactful, motivating message delivered clearly, written with the reader in mind. If you want your book to make a difference, you don't want the message to take the back seat to a faux-academic persona.

Furthermore, you want to avoid coming across as impersonal. The use of an unnatural voice, by which I mean one that goes against the grain of normal speech, is distracting and is often received as contrived. Readers will get the impression that you are trying to be someone you are not, which could prove damaging to your reputation over the lifetime of your book.

Okay, pause. How did that last paragraph feel to you? Was it a little jarring? Did it seem slightly out of place and disingenuous? I hope your answers are "yes" because that was me switching to a more "writerly" voice to "sound smart." The effect is that I just sound weird because I wouldn't speak that way if you met me. This is a book—*my* book—not a research paper!

Don't be afraid to have fun and say what you really think and do so in a way that feels true to you. Editors are pretty keen about identifying your true voice and helping it shine in the written word. Trust them to help you look good. They're trusting you to bring the heart.

There are important aspects to writing and good style, but given that not all authors who write good books are native English speakers, it is really a moot point for *this* book. The only requirement is that you communicate your thoughts as clearly as possible.

BE OPEN TO INSPIRATION

I know we just spent nine chapters designing the perfect book plan—your success blueprint. But I have something to tell you… It's not the only element to writing a good book. This road map is meant as a guide; it's actually the back-up strategy.

Having a foolproof plan makes it so much easier to write because you know what to say before you sit down to say it. The thing is, there is something that happens as you settle into your work and get into a flow state: inspiration.

As the author, you are the authority. You bring the magic and the message to your reader through your words. However, you are not alone in this book-creation journey. You are in co-creation with the Universe to bring out a message that feels bigger than you.

I experienced this with *Facing Racism*. I put everything I had into that book and promised myself that I would show up and be willing to share whatever message needed to be shared in that moment. When the book was done and I finally reread it after publishing, I found myself *shocked* by what was there. There were things I had no recollection of writing.

Some will say that it's because I was in a heightened state of "flow" and I wasn't storing any of what I was writing in those moments. I like to think that there is an element of divine inspiration that assists us in any purpose driven act of love, rebellion, or creativity. Whatever you call it, when it comes over you, run with it. Even if it's not exactly what's on the blueprint.

Even this book took a slightly different shape from the original outline as I was writing. There were things that seemed more relevant to talk about after I started, things I hadn't considered before. This will probably happen to you. Don't block your intuition. Instead, leave a note for yourself or your editor to review those sections to check them against your purpose statement and the overall flow of the book. If what you've written doesn't work, you can always fall back on your outline. The most important thing for you to do is keep writing toward your goal and not stop.

ACTIVITY

This may a chapter on writing, but the first exercise I have for you is a bit of close reading. Choose a nonfiction book that you enjoyed reading and open it to one of your favorite chapters. Read this chapter and take notes about the following writing elements:

- Author voice and tone (How does it sound and feel?)
- Use of storytelling/narrative (Who is involved? Where does it start? What details are included? Where and how is the story resolved?)
- Chapter Structure (Can you identify the main points of the chapter? How does the chapter start and end?)

The Second exercise I'd like you to attempt is outlining a chapter of your own. It doesn't have to be a real chapter in the book you intend to write, so don't feel like you have to figure out your whole book if you haven't yet. Choose a topic that you could write about. Write a purpose statement asserting what you want your reader to learn about this topi by the end of the chapter. Finally use the following outline to plan it your chapter. You don't have to write the chapter, but using full sentences is beneficial.

Intro

o Story (ideally of when you or a client learned, applied, or failed to apply the topic)

   a) Where were you? What were you trying to do (that wasn't working?) What was your belief?

   b) What did you do? What happened?

   c) What was the result?

o Context (Explicitly state the main idea of the story. Why are you telling it?)

o Preview topic (What is this story about? What will you discuss in the rest of the chapter)

Body

o Point 1 (First core concept)

   a) Common misconception

   b) Truth

   c) Your lesson

   d) (Simple) Example

   e) Reflection

o Point 2 (Second core concept)

   a) Your lesson

   b) (Simple) Example

   c) Reflection

Conclusion

o Transition statement

o Core takeaways

   a)

   b)

o Action item (Give readers an activity)

EDITING SECRETS

What's the first thing you think of when you hear the word "editing?" Is it someone behind a desk, sitting with his glasses halfway down his nose and a red pen scrawling all over your printed manuscript? Is it a grammar-obsessed librarian with a pencil tucked behind her ear smiling outwardly at you, but inwardly ready to tell you all the ways you've misused or misspelled a word?

When I ask authors what they think editing is, I usually get one of two images. The first is of them painstakingly rewriting the entire book over from page one. The second is of them handing over their manuscript to someone who abhors creativity so that that person can tell them all of the ways they suck at writing. If these images make you cringe, you're lucky—they make me quake with a blend of disgust and disbelief.

Of course, these images come from a collection of authors' horror stories about how much they had to cut and from a lifetime of educators critiquing papers and demanding students rewrite them. In my experience as an editor, none of the images conjured in the first two paragraphs are what editing is about.

In his memoir, *On Writing*, Stephen King said, "When you write a book, you spend day after day scanning and identifying the trees. When you're done, you have to step back and look at the forest." To me, this is what editing is about. When you're writing, you spend so much time meticulously exploring in the woods, marking tree after tree and noting every boulder, log, and foxhole you come across until you have a complete view of the locale. Editing, on the other hand, is pulling back to see the big picture.

I said before that writing is a way of conveying your ideas, like thinking onto the page. The more orderly your thoughts, the clearer your writing will be. Editing is a process through which we take this collection of ideas and turn it into a coherent, cohesive body that holds itself up. It involves multiple steps, not just fixing grammar and spelling.

As a busy change-leader, I fully expect you to hire professional editors to take your manuscript from rough draft to publishing-ready. Even so, I thought it would be useful to outline the editing process and clarify your role as the author.

Every good book goes through a comprehensive editing process that evaluates content and analyzes tone, style, clarity, accuracy, form, and adherence to style guides. Each of these qualities gets approached in one of four main types of edit: developmental edit, line edit, copyedit, and proofread. (A fifth type would be interior formatting, but that is more of a design element, and will not be included in this breakdown.)

DEVELOPMENTAL EDITING

Developmental editing is the first phase of the book editing process. At this level, editors read your manuscript and provide a thorough evaluation of your work at the content level. This high-level critique focuses on the big picture to determine what your book may need before publication. At this phase, it's all about assessing for completeness, organization, value, and purpose.

A developmental editor will be looking to answer questions like, "Does this book feel complete?" "Does each chapter feel complete?" "Is it focused?" "Is it engaging?" "Is the right content in the right places?" "Does each chapter accomplish the purpose?" and "If I were the ideal reader, where do I feel confused or like the work is lacking?"

Depending on who your editor is, you will receive this edit as a comprehensive cover letter combined with in-line comments and directives for you to implement or the editor will make certain changes on your behalf using a tracking feature. In the latter case, the feedback would be a combination of clarifying questions and explanations as to why they made certain changes. Your job is to review their notes and changes for approval and direction.

The reason this is the first level of editing is because this is where your book will see the most comprehensive and substantial changes. If you need to include more stories or information for your book to make sense and feel whole, this is the edit that will catch that. If you spend too much time in one area and not enough in another, this is where that will get noted.

In terms of price, this can be the most expensive stage of editing because of the level of involvement with the work. A good developmental editor is a close reader who cannot only assess what's being said, but what the author meant to say, whether they should say it, and where they should say it in the text. The developmental editor may ask a lot of the author, but it's all with the goal of making the book better.

LINE EDITING

Sometimes called substantive editing[1], this type of edit is second-level, and the first to deal with linguistics and style. It's a step in between developmental and copyediting in that it deals with clarity and organization but at the paragraph and sentence level. Further, it examines your syntax and word choice to make your writing lean and powerful.

This is the edit where your writing stops looking like a choppy collection of ideas and more like the well-organized, fluid strings of thought that you would expect of a published work. If you are unsure about variances in your voice, this is where that is usually captured. If you use a lot of passive voice, filler words, adjectives, run-on sentences, and sentence fragments, your editor will fix that here.

When I conduct line edits, I typically look for quality in four categories: Simplicity, Clarity, Elegance, Evocativeness. These qualities are outlined by former editor of the *Wall Street Journal* Shani Raja in many of his teachings. As they apply to editing, they prompt questions like, "Is this piece of writing easy to read/uncomplex?" "Is it transparent and easily understood?" "Is it orderly, stylish, and graceful?" and, finally, "Is it powerful? Does the language evoke feelings?"

The developmental edit is all about what you said, and the line edit is all about how well you said it.

COPYEDITING

Copyediting is the most well-known and misunderstood type of editing. There are many good writers who fancy themselves copyeditors, but many don't exactly live up to this claim, and here's why. Copyediting is more than spelling, grammar, and punctuation. Yes, those are three of the core elements, but this edit also assesses for accuracy and consistency in elements such as punctuation, enumeration, naming and form conventions, and citations. In digital media, this can include verifying that hyperlinks work appropriately. This task can also include fact-checking and verifying that references are accurate.

This level of edit is *not* for the faint of heart. This editor *must* have an eye for detail, a love for the art of nitpicking, and a strong understanding of the varying rules of writing. For example, your copyeditor would know the difference between how *The Chicago Manual of Style* and *The Associated Press Stylebook* (the two major guides in the US) handle numbers, including the different rules for statistics, time, and money. They would know the differences in how each guide prefers to capitalize subheadings.

During this edit, you can expect a lot of small detail changes that would be very tedious to read through. As the author, your role is usually to read through the document without the markup turned off. If you approve the changes, you can then accept all of the changes. At this point, you do not want to add any new content because it will not get edited unless you specifically ask your editor to do another pass through new material.

PROOFREADING

This one is exactly what you think it is: checking spelling, punctuation, typos, and all of the little details that may have been missed. If you thought your copyeditor was good, proofreaders are the unsung heroes who catch the most persistent of errors, like open quotes that should be closed, unintended missing letters, or unexplained bold letters.

Your proofreader doesn't assess content, clarity, style, or accuracy of facts or numbers. They make sure that if you have chosen to spell out all numerals under 100 per *CMoS* with the exception of times and chapter titles, it is done consistently throughout the book, on every page, line by line. You can think of proofreaders as the ones who make sure you don't embarrass yourself with small avoidable mistakes.

This is an edit that most authors can recognize the importance of because, honestly, readers are unforgiving when they find errors in books. I've seen readers give a book one star on Amazon because they found four typos in the first *200 pages!* Your role in this stage is the same as with the copyedit, although at this stage I would strongly encourage you to pay close attention to detail. Avoid getting lost in the excitement of seeing your book almost finished. Even experienced, well-paid proofreaders can miss things. As much as you'll want to blame them when a reader finds an error, the public will only ever see and blame you. It's your book; you own it.

Now that you know what goes into editing a book, you must be exhausted! (I am!) Okay, seriously though, there is a lot of work that happens after you finish your initial manuscript. So much that, after going through this process themselves, many authors opt to leave the bulk of their editing to professionals because it is so time-consuming. I would recommend that you follow their example.

It's a well-known fact of writing that even the best writers should not self-edit. There are several books on how to edit your own work. I've read a few and do my own edits on smaller projects. However, any time I write a book, I hire an editor. Likewise, in my work with clients, I rely on a team of qualified professionals to ensure quality, timely edits. (Once an editor has done two rounds of edits on a manuscript, it is best to have another do the proofread because they'll have fresher eyes.)

In my experience, authors get the best results when they let the professionals do the heavier lifting at this phase. Think of it this way. When you need to get your car fixed, you see a mechanic. When you need your toilet replaced, you call a plumber. When you need a socket replaced, you call an electrician. If you wouldn't trust yourself with these jobs, why would you trust yourself with your book?

TITLE, DESCRIPTION, AND COVER DESIGN

Before moving on, I wanted to take a second and acknowledge how much information you've absorbed. Not only have you learned how to write your book, but you've also earned two more stars on our makeshift book proposal checklist: a sample chapter and production details.

1. Working Title ____
2. Hook or Tagline ★
3. Book Description ____
4. Target Market ★
5. Market Analysis (why your book is relevant) ★
6. Marketing Plan ____
7. Author Bio ____
8. Chapter Summary ★
9. Production Details (length, format, completion date, etc.) ★
10. Sample Chapter ★

We have just a few blank spots to fill in, and this is the chapter where we cross the finish line.

So you've written the book. (Yes, I know you haven't literally written your book yet because you're here reading this one). Now it's time to package it up and get ready to share your new baby with the world. But, like all babies, it needs a name and some stellar new clothes. This chapter is all about what goes on the outside of your book (selling).

NAMING YOUR BOOK

Most authors think they know the names of their book before they start writing. While it can be good to have a working title, I always advise waiting until the very end before choosing a final title. The reason is that, before you write the book, you don't really know what you have. Sometimes the title an author chooses before they write the book is the one that they wish they had written, when in reality what they have is slightly different. I remember the conversation I had with my editor when we were choosing a title for my previous book.

The whole time I was working on the book, the project title was *The End of Racism*. It seemed bold, confident, striking, and true to my intentions as an author. While my editor agreed on those points, she had some concerns.

"It's a nice, strong title," she said, "but it doesn't feel like the book you've actually written."

"I'm not sure I follow," I said.

"When you choose a title, you are essentially making your readers a promise, right?"

"Right."

"Ending racism is a really big promise. I don't mean to say you don't deliver a compelling case. I just mean that what you've shared feels more like the start of a conversation than solving a complex problem."

She had a point. When I thought back over my actual content, and where my reader was positioned, it really was more of the start of a conversation about race. On top of that, racism, as defined in the book and within a sociological perspective, is not necessarily the problem I addressed.

I really liked the way my title sounded, but I didn't want to make a lofty claim about ending racism if that's absolutely not what I was doing. She gave me "homework" that week to come up with three to five alternatives that we could workshop. I don't remember all of them, but I know that *Facing Racism* was the first one and *Facing Each Other* was another.

"No," she said to the second option when I brought it up.

"Why not?" I asked. "My book is really about learning to come together and open up dialogues."

I could see from the look on her face that she was trying to find a nice way to say it sucked. "Yes, but *Facing Each Other* totally eliminates the attractive part about race and racial justice. Honestly, I would personally recommend the top option on this list. I also love that your first revision is literally the best. It makes a good promise without overreaching and it has the rhyming factor that makes it memorable."

Obviously, we know which title ended up on the cover, but my editor's reasoning is what I want to call your attention to. Your book title is both your best marketing hook and a promise to your readers. You don't want to create a title that doesn't match the scope of your book. This is why it's so important to revisit your title *after* you've written your book.

There is another important reason for waiting until the end, and this one may make more sense. Most authors who choose a title before writing haven't done any of the planning we've covered in this book. So they haven't taken the time to really get into the heads of their ideal readers. As such, the working title often hasn't been optimized to be irresistible to their ideal readers—instead, it can tend to sound like whatever they thought sounded cool at the time.

Do you remember when I used the title of Gary Chapman's

The 5 Love Languages: The Secret to Love that Lasts to reverse-engineer the ideal reader's specific problem and heart's desire? The only reason that worked is because the title of that book has been optimized to speak directly to Chapman's ideal reader.

You want to do the same when choosing your title and subtitle. Remember that the title is not just the catchy memorable name of your book-baby, but your number one most important marketing tool. Your title is for selling! To craft a good title, you want to make good use of your reader's RSP and RHD, because those are phrases that you've determined are already in your reader's head. Follow the guidance below to craft your book's perfect title:

Book Title

This is derived from your RHD. It should be snappy and easy to read and recognize. You may have something clever in mind that could work. Just remember that the goal is to make your book instantly recognizable to your ideal reader .

- Ex. *Facing Racism*
- Ex. *Traffic Secrets*
- Ex. *Write Your Book in No Time*

Book Subtitle

This comes from your RSP. You want it to be brief and easy to say in one breath. It may generally be "How to [solve problem]."

- Ex. *The Guide to Overcoming Unconscious Bias and Hidden Prejudice to Be a Part of the Change*
- Ex. *The Underground Playbook for Filling Your Websites and Funnels with Your Dream Customers*

- Ex. *The Entrepreneur's Guide to Finishing a High-Impact Book While Running Your Business*

No matter what you choose for your title, as long as it's optimized with your ideal reader's language, it will be instantly more attractive—which is paramount if you want your book to make a difference in people's lives.

DESCRIBING YOUR BOOK

Think about the last time you were scrolling through books on Amazon or in your local bookstore and a book caught your attention. What was the first thing you noticed about it? Probably the title and cover art, right? Once you picked up the book and read the title, what was the very next thing you did? You scrolled down or flipped it over to read the description, right?

Think about that sequence: Art > Title > Description. If you shop this way, this is actually because this is how nearly all book buyers shop. What this means for you is that, if you want to sell your book (sell readers on your book), your powerful selling tool behind your title is your book description. Ninety-nine percent of shoppers make their decision based on what's written there, before ever opening the book. If you get them to open the book, that means you've done a good job with the description. They are already mentally buying your book.

Because it is such a crucial part of your reader's shopping experience, you want to make sure that, like the title, your book description is optimized to *sell*. You are not merely describing here. You are trying to persuade someone to make a purchasing decision, and the way you do that is by positioning your book as the one thing they cannot live without in that moment. You accomplish this by elaborating on the RSP and RHD.

In marketing terms, you build up the reader's emotions by

describing their pain points, showing them their dream come true, and then positioning your book as the vehicle to get from pain to pleasure. One of the biggest mistakes new authors make is that they try to talk about all of the great things that are inside the book. This is wrong not because the material is bad, but because not all of that material is geared toward selling your book. You want to *show* the reader that you get them and their wish and that your book has a solution for them. Here is a breakdown of the core elements of a solid book description:

HEADLINE (around 10 – 15 words)

- Write a hook that captures the ideal reader's heart's desire.
- Make it punchy and attention-grabbing.
- Try to include a keyword that your reader would search on Google.

DESCRIPTION (around 50 – 100 words)

- Describes the problem in the reader's words.
- Describes your ideal reader's heart's desire.
- Remember to focus on the emotion.
- How does it feel in the problem? What would life look like without it?
- Introduce yourself with a credibility sentence or less.

BENEFITS (50-120 words)

- List benefits in bullet point format (4 – 5).
- Focus on the outcomes your reader will get, not the work or features.

- Remember the benefits should be things your reader wants from their level of awareness/understanding.
- Write bullet points in parallel construction.

SUMMARY (about 30 words)

- Appeal to the heart's desire.
- Include a simple call to action.
- If possible compare your book to similar bestsellers and name drop known authors.

In total, your book description should be between 200 and 250 words. If this feels like copywriting, that's because it is! Copywriting is all about writing text that persuades people to take action, and that is exactly your goal here. You are not writing just to talk about the great things inside your book. You're writing to show the reader the life-changing results they're going to get from reading it. For an example, take another look at the description for this book. See if you can identify the elements above at play:

> Writing a book sounds like a lot of work. But what if it didn't have to be?
>
> Thousands of new books are published every year by entrepreneurs, coaches, and thought-leaders like you. You may be wondering how they're all doing it. You've had it in your head to get one out "soon," but it's a big commitment—also confusing and overwhelming for a first-time author. Between managing projects, serving your clients, and having time for you, it feels like there's never a good time.
>
> It'd be great if you had a clear roadmap that makes

writing easy for a total beginner with a full schedule. If you could get it organized and written without missing work—or worse, staying up late after a long day—you would have it done.

Well, consider this your new playbook! In *Write Your Book in No Time*, editor, writing coach, and bestselling author, Andrae D. Smith, Jr. nearly a decade of writing knowledge into a simple, twelve-step framework for planning, writing, and publishing your book. You'll learn:

• How to easily fit book-work into your schedule without overloading
• Which tasks will actually help you finish, and which ones to stop immediately
• Proven strategies for writing great content efficiently
• Easy tips to ensure your new book is irresistible to your readers

If you're a passion-driven coach or expert ready to turn your experience into a meaningful book without wasting time or money, this is the breakthrough you've been looking for. Get it today!

CREATE YOUR SHORT BIO

As a successful entrepreneur, you're no stranger to talking about yourself and what you do. It's likely that you have one or more bios already, so I won't spend too much time here. I just want to provide a little guidance on how to optimize yours for the back of your book. Unlike on your website or your About the Author page, you only have about seventy to eighty words to make the best impression possible.

To write an impactful bio, you want to keep it lean. Stick to three or four sentences of about twenty words in length. The first sentence is your personal introduction and should contain your title or work, your name, and a prominent accolade if you have one. In the next sentence, you want to talk about your change or transformation.

This is a before-and-after look that showcases your triumph over a problem or a discovery of your passion. The third sentence should highlight what you do now. This is your "I help" statement with the result you get clients now. Finally, if you include a fourth sentence, this is where you can include any prominent media appearances.

Take a look at two different versions of my author bio. The first one is short and focuses on telling my expertise. The second one follows the formula above. Which do you think is stronger and more evocative, and why?

Bio 1

Bestselling author Andrae D. Smith, Jr. has worked as a writing mentor, coach, and book editor since 2014, after studying creative writing and technical editing in college. In 2020, Andrae wrote and published *Facing Racism* in just three months. He now devotes his time to helping passionate coaches, healers, and movement leaders write books that transform lives.

Bio 2

Andrae D. Smith, Jr. is a part-time freelance editor turned #1 bestselling author, book-writing coach, and the founder of Illuminated Authors. After a fateful car accident in 2019 convinced him to leave his mundane retail job, Andrae chose to use his talents full-time and build a new, purpose-driven life. He now devotes his skills and passion to helping inspired coaches and movement leaders make a bigger impact by writing books that transform lives.

Each version has its own strengths and drawbacks. In the first version, it's very clear that I've been working in this field for a long time. It also highlights my accomplishment in becoming a bestselling author and in writing my book in a short amount of time. It also ends on the "what I do now" statement. The major criticism I have is that it's not very compelling. It looks as though I've had a straightforward journey to this point. There is no hook or story.

The second version does not elaborate on my expertise as much and leaves little room to highlight some of the roles I've filled and my writing accomplishments. I could have brought attention to how many authors I've worked with over the years. However, what it lacks in background, this version makes up for in character and story. It introduces me and my accomplishments in becoming an author and highlights the work I do, all in the first sentence. The second sentence tells a story that adds drama, intrigue, and inspiration. The final sentence closes it with the "what I do now" statement, only, with the added story quality, this same sentence packs a bigger punch. This bio as a whole introduces me while inviting people to ask questions.

Arguably, the first one is more concise, but the second one is more compelling. The second one entices readers to want to get to know me in a way they can in just seventy-four words. They will be more engaged with my stories and my message, and they will probably visit my About the Author page for a full story.

This is what you want from your bio—for people to get curious, lean in, and want to know more about you. You don't need to give every detail about yourself up front. Readers don't want you to, anyway. Instead focus on credibility factors and points that make you relatable to your ideal readers. Turn your bio into a story. Stories are about movement and change. So when you're revising your bio, think, "What is my story of transformation?" and "How can I summarize it in just three sentences?"

COVER ART

The last thing I want to discuss in this chapter is your cover art. I saved this for last simply because, unless you are creating your own cover, you will be outsourcing this to a graphic designer, ideally one who has experience creating book covers for your genre.

The first thing you should know is that, when it comes to cover art, you get what you pay for, generally speaking. If you hire a designer for $20 or less, you can expect an unoriginal, uninspiring cover. On the other hand, you can get something truly beautiful for between $200 and $300. For something truly custom, you may find yourself paying as much as $500 or more. No matter the price, always ask to see a portfolio and have some conversation with an artist before hiring them. Nothing is more frustrating than working with someone you can't get along with.

What do you want in a cover? Your cover can look however you want it to. However, I've found that it's useful to pay attention to genre and trends. For example, if you're writing a book on spellcraft for modern witches set to release in October of 2021, then you may consider a black cover with gold, silver, or white fonts. You'd also probably want lunar imagery and elements that call back to nature or a goddess. By contrast, if your book is about mindset and productivity, you might avoid the black background and occult imagery in favor of something more contemporary and minimalistic.

Ultimately, you'll tell your cover designer what you like based on your personal taste and branding. Just be mindful of the imagery and the messages it will send to your ideal reader. For instance, if you're in real estate or finance, it can be to your advantage to have a more "corporate" look because that's what readers expect of the genre. I had to make a similar choice when choosing a cover for this book—whether to go corporate and straightforward or to add elements of magic (which would be on-brand for me).

Personally, I love magic, so when my designer, Emily, showed me her proposals, I was completely awestruck. They were gorgeous and evocative, just like I wanted. But some just didn't match the tone this book needed. It's a more straightforward book, and it needed a cover that felt both fresh and classic. I wanted it to feel exactly like what you would expect to see from a traditional publisher, but unique enough to stand apart and command attention when presented as a part of a lineup. I believe the words I gave Emily were, "Simple, elegant, and striking."

No matter your preferences, always remember to be clear, confident, respectful, and open-minded when working with a designer. Don't be afraid to ask for exactly what you want, but remember that designers are creatives and will likely add their own flair on top of your ideas. Be open to pleasant surprises. The cover of this book is actually nothing like what I had envisioned when I filled out the intake form. There was a cover proposal that turned out to be almost a direct match for what I thought I wanted... until I saw this one and fell in love instantly. That's what can happen when you keep your options open.

If you and your designer aren't exactly seeing eye-to-eye on direction, understand that this is normal. Be supportive of their vision, even when holding firm to your expectations. Whenever possible, remain encouraging and express gratitude. The more pleasant the experience is working with you, the better the work they do and the more they will want to meet your needs. For the creative person, getting to the perfect cover can be like solving a puzzle, and as they get positive feedback from you, they are encouraged to keep going until you respond with, "Wow! That's it!"

Whether you work with one designer or a whole design team, remember that it's a team effort and you have the same goal. Have patience during the creative process. The value of a good cover is too significant for you to rush the process. Trust the process and work with your book partners, not over or against them.

By now you should have a better understanding of how your book's exterior design plays into the book's attractiveness. A traditional publishing house will typically have an entire team of marketing experts working out what elements to include in the title, subtitle, and artwork because it can be that important. In a world where thousands of books are published and competing for reader attention, you need a cover that will stop the natural scanning activity that people's eyes do.

You want to hook them and never let them go. Each element is designed to create a persuasive experience for your ideal reader so that they become completely enchanted by you. You may think that your title, book description, or artwork feel a little bland, or you may love them. What matters, though, is that when your reader sees it, it sticks out like a ray from heaven. Your book is the answer to their prayers, and that's what they need to feel when they find it.

ACTIVITY

This chapter's activity has two parts. For the first part, you must analyze the titles of two books you own to see if you can identify the ideal reader, their specific problem, and their heart's desire. Then practice creating your own based on your ideal reader's RSP and RHD.

In the second part, you will evaluate the book description of one of these books to see what elements the author used to *sell* you on their book. Then practice by creating a draft of your own.

WRITER'S BLOCK OR WRITING BLOCKS?

> Cellists don't have cellist block. Gardeners don't have gardener's block. TV hosts do not have TV host block. But writers have claimed all the blocks, and we think [writer's block is] a real thing."
>
> — NEIL GAIMAN (*HUFFPOST* INTERVIEW, 2015)

A few years ago, I was sitting on my bed reading from a book of spells I had bought from Barnes & Noble earlier that day. It was October, and "spooky season" was in full effect. Two pillar candles and a small bedside lamp were my only light source, and the smell of sandalwood hung in the air from my incense. At that time, I was deeply immersed in the idea of myself as a wizard in training and had built a good-sized collection of books for "study."

Bzzzt. My cellphone buzzed on the nightstand next to me: a new text from Crystal. "OMG! Guess what?"

"What?" I replied.

"I'm writing tonight!"

"No way! I'll believe it when I see the words. [roll eyes emoji]" She had been in one of her writing dry spells for weeks, and no matter how many times I tried to encourage her or help her out, I couldn't get her to put more than a few words on the page. It was hardly worth sharing, so we paused our meetings.

"Okay, fine. I'll send it to you tomorrow!"

"I'll be waiting. You got this."

The next day, I checked my inbox for Crystal's email. It was there! She had written something, at least enough for her to back up her excitement. I opened it to find five pages of content she had created. It didn't seem attached to the chapter that she had left off on, but it was good.

On Friday, we got on a video call using my meeting ID (what a perfect example of an irrelevant detail…). I congratulated her on her achievement and let her explain her scene to me. One of my favorite things as a coach is listening to my authors talk about their projects. They sit up straighter and start talking really fast. They never notice it, but they always smile through the whole thing.

When she was finished, I shared a few of my thoughts from reading her piece and then started coaching. "How did it feel?" I asked.

"Really great. It's like I finally had this massive breakthrough."

"Certainly. How did this all come up for you? What happened?"

She told me how she was cooking dinner, cutting up vegetables, and she got a flashback of a time in her grandma's kitchen when she was a kid. She remembered all of the feelings and thought it would be great to capture that. She went the whole evening holding on to those feelings until she had a free moment to pull out her journal. She started writing her memories and, before she knew what was happening, she stopped being herself and became her main character. The memories stopped being just hers and became rumination from this fictional person.

"So when you realized you were feeling nostalgic, what made you decide it was time to write?"

"I don't know… it just came to me and it made sense. I wasn't thinking about my story until after I started writing. Then *this* (she waved her arms in front of her) happened."

"Do you feel like you'll be able to keep this up?" I asked.

"I don't know. I have to wait for inspiration to find me and then milk it for as long as possible."

I wanted to push her a little to write more deliberately, but I wanted to respect her creative process too. George R. R. Martin says that some writers are gardeners and never really know how the seeds they planted will grow, and I took that to apply to a person's writing process as well. So I backed off and gave Crystal some encouragement to keep sharing as she writes so we would have stuff to talk about. Sometimes creative dialogue could keep the inspiration flowing a little longer.

The thing about Crystal was that she only wrote when she felt inspired. Sometimes she could write for days or weeks. Other times, she could be "blocked" and do no substantial writing for months. This sounds absurd, but Crystal's case is not as uncommon as you'd think.

There is a pervasive myth within the writing community that there exists this thing called "writer's block." It allegedly happens when a writer sits down at their desk, opens their project, and finds themselves unable to write. Ultimately they spend the session typing and deleting their first sentence or browsing the internet, all the while praying to the gods of writing (Apollo, Thoth, Hermes, Bragi…) for a sprinkle of inspiration. Often these prayers go unanswered and writers treat it like, as Gaiman put it, they've been cursed.

I've faced this experience many times in my writing and editing career. When I was a young writer, there would be long stretches where I simply didn't write. People would ask me why, and the only thing I could tell them was that I wasn't "feeling" it. Back then, I just accepted my fate because I had heard more experienced writers say things like, "It happens to all of us. Just put the project away for a while, go live life, and wait for inspiration to strike again." They usually followed that with, "Keep a notebook handy so that when it happens, you're not unprepared."

I actually spent many years holding on to this belief and reciting this advice with my writing mentees, trying to be supportive. I didn't realize until later in my career that I was doing more harm than good because my mentees were paying me monthly to basically enable the same habits and beliefs that caused them not to write. My role then was as a writing coach, not a productivity coach, so I thought it was fine, until I started helping people who wanted to get across the finish line on their books.

After working with nearly seventy authors who've written and published their books, I've come to realize that writer's block actually doesn't exist. What *does* exist are writ-*ing* blocks. These are situations and conditions that cause a writer to feel stuck. There is a small but essential difference between the two. In the former case, you declare that you're blocked and the only way out is to stop writing until this mystical blockage clears up. You may not even know what needs clearing, but you wait. In the latter, there is something real with a root cause that has created the effect of your stuck-ness.

By addressing the cause, you can clear the block. In the rest of this chapter, I want to take a quick look at six of the most common instances of blocks that I've encountered with my authors, even while actively in my coaching program.

I. GETTING STUCK AT THE INTRO OR CONCLUSION

At the beginning of the year, I had a client who was excelling in my program. She had finished the development phase two weeks early and had written nearly half of her manuscript in the week after that. She and I had worked together before, so she was familiar with the process, making it easier for her to plow through content like it was nothing.

We got on our weekly progress call one Monday and she told me she was feeling a little stuck when it came to writing chapter 1. Like most authors, she wasn't exactly sure how to start. I like to call this "fear of first impressions." It's generally accepted among writers that if a reader opens your book, it's not sold yet. They are going to judge you by the quality of your first few sentences. (Talk about pressure!) Naturally, she would be nervous.

What I've found is that the fear of first impressions isn't the only problem authors face. It's the last impressions too. Many authors are afraid to tackle their conclusion chapter because they don't want their books to fall flat (another valid concern). Unfortunately, this fear manifests as a writing block.

To curb this, I typically tell authors to save both for last, to write out of order. The reason these sections are harder to write is simply because you most likely don't know enough about the book or you haven't settled into your voice as the author. Writing other chapters first can help you.

If you reach the end and still struggle with one or both of these sections, look back at the goals mentioned in the chapter on content. Pick three things that you would like your reader to know before and after reading—or three goals you would like them to achieve. Then assign them each one talking point or story and just write. Don't worry about writing the perfect opening or transition; that will come when you revise it.

II. CAN'T THINK OF GOOD STORIES

I hear this all the time from authors in the self-help genre: "I don't have any good stories!" or "How do I know which stories to tell?" This was the case for another of my authors from early in the year. Her book was more technical, and she wasn't really sure how to infuse story into her writing. She just knew she didn't want her book to be boring.

What I told her was to think of writing like having a conversation. In regular speech, we are constantly making associations and relating topics back to things that have happened to us. If you were talking to someone about a topic, what's one thing that has happened in real life that you can think of to clarify the point or that simply feels related?

On our next call, this client and I talked about a couple of the topics, and instinctively she started telling me about one of her clients and what they did and how the client struggled. When she was done, I told her, "By the way, there's your story for this chapter."

"OMG! I hope you're recording!" she said, laughing.

Fortunately, I had remembered to push the record button at the start of our meeting. If you struggle to think up a relevant story while writing, try pretending you're in conversation. If you're not used to flexing that imaginative muscle, go have a real conversation. Something will come to you.

One last thing to keep in mind is that you don't need a story in every chapter or even for every point. Sometimes it is enough just to give the information. I'll show you in the next point.

III. GETTING STUCK IN AN EDITING CYCLE

The most common trap I see authors make is trying to edit while they are writing. They do this thing psychologically where they think, "I could have said this better," and they start rewriting things before they've finished the chapter. Some authors get a little stalled and lose their trains of thought, so they reread the chapter to remember where they were going. On the surface, this act is innocuous, but what ends up happening is these authors start questioning what they wrote.

Instead of getting clarity to write their next paragraph, they start seeing all of their mistakes, from typos to stray thoughts. Instinctively, they think they have to fix those things right then "because [their] brains won't let them move on now that they've seen it." This is normal, and even I encounter this when I write. There is a desire to get things right, fostered by years of being told to revise before turning in a piece of writing.

Remember, no one else is going to see your rough draft except for your editor, who you'll pay a lot of money specifically to catch all of these things *for* you. I'm not saying to give your editor sloppy work. What I am saying is that you must practice writing forward, even though there are errors. Yes, you could have been more concise. Yes, there *is* a better word. No, that sentence doesn't make sense right now. That's okay. Keep writing to the end.

Writing and editing are two different cognitive functions that engage the different hemispheres of the brain. You can't write in flow state if you keep stopping to edit because you never allow yourself to surrender control. Flow happens when you are at ease. Editorial work is all about being critical. The two do not align. Your inner critic is going to want to change things in the moment. You have to promise that part of you to simply be patient. It will have the opportunity to tear up your document—*after* you've written it. Not before.

IV. ALLOWING DISTRACTIONS

I mentioned distractions in the chapter on time. This is, hands down, the number one reason authors don't hit their goals and finish their books on time. Distractions happen for two reasons: habit and fear. If you're not writing, it is either because you haven't flexed your focus muscle enough to be able to work for an extended period or you have an underlying resistance to the task.

I set out to write and edit this book in thirty days. I knew I could have a draft written in about three, but it took me seven. What happened? Simply put, life. I promised my readers that I would not stop my regular life to make room for this project, since that is how my prospects will experience the work. As such, there were things I needed to attend to such as emails, messenger conversations, sales calls, coaching calls, grocery shopping, laundry, cleaning, babysitting, exercising...

All of these things need attention in order for me to lead a balanced and successful life. The problem was not the tasks, but how efficiently I did them and when I did them. I know there were two days where I allowed meetings to occur during my designated writing time. I didn't protect my boundary, and I had to make up that time.

Remember, don't pay for today with tomorrow's time. Tomorrow has its own expenses. If you're allowing distractions today, you are imposing a block on today's productivity.

V. NOT RUNNING THE PLAN

This is less common, but it is a reason some authors face writing blocks. The reason I teach the writing process the way I do and then have authors write before editing is because it systemizes the work. When you follow the steps in order, you build clarity and get used to taking small, meaningful action.

What sometimes happens, though, is an author will begin the writing phase with enthusiasm, and then after their first session or two, they slow down.

They get confident enough in their progress and start to see themselves crossing the finish line, and instead of pushing through, they start to veer off. In track-and-field, runners are told not to slow down or look over their shoulders as they approach the finish line. Instead they need to look straight, "dig deep," and "run like hell" until they are on the other side. Put simply, they need to stay the course.

When you go to write your book, you will have a plan. The plan is designed for you to succeed. The only reason you should deviate from your plan is that you've found a better strategy. When you deviate from the plan (except to allow flow), you are looking over your shoulder instead of keeping your eyes on your goal. You start to veer and end up in lanes you hadn't planned on—and that is why you get confused.

Attitude, strategy, and implementation are the pillars upon which this method or philosophy of writing sits. You need all three to be successful.

VI. IMPOSTER SYNDROME

"Who am I to write this book?" That's a question every new author must face, and it comes up over and over again. When many of us decide to write self-help books, it is because we have the goal of *helping* someone else. There is a lot of excitement around creating these books because we know that they will make a difference for someone who needs it.

Then we start writing and running into writing blocks. Our ideas don't flow. Our sentences are choppy. Our books don't feel like the books we've read—what if they aren't as good as other books? Why would anyone buy from us?

Before we know it, we start asking ourselves all of these

qualifying—or rather, disqualifying—questions. Because that is the goal in the moment. The brain is like a supercomputer that runs programs all day. When you insert a directive to find reasons you aren't qualified to write a book, it will do so.

When this happens, the first thing you want to do is stop the program. Notice when you start to doubt yourself and feel yourself spinning out instead of writing. Take a breath and notice one thing in your environment with each of your senses. This is a simple grounding technique to calm the anxious nervous system.

Next, take out a piece of paper. A computer works, but pen and paper is better for this. Create three vertical columns by drawing two lines down the page. The left and right columns should be wider than the middle. The middle column can be about half an inch (one fingernail) wide. At the top of the columns, write: Belief, T/F, and Evidence.

On this paper, you're going to literally write out all of the negative thoughts, beliefs, and worries that come to your head in the left column. Write these things honestly as they come to you. Don't judge it, don't revise it. Just let it be. Once you've written all of the thoughts (five-ten is pretty normal), you'll read them to yourself and ask, "Is this statement about me true or false? Write T or F in the middle column. Finally, when you've evaluated each statement, go down the list one more time. For anything that you put a T by, use the right column to write out your proof or evidence.

What most authors find when they go through this is that they actually have *no proof* or that what they think is evidence is actually not. For example, a common thing authors say is, "Well, I've never written a book before." My response when we do this on a call is usually something like, "Yeah, and tell me, were you a college graduate before or after you studied? ... There's a first time for everything. Everyone who's written and published had to write their first book before becoming an author."

Find out your limiting beliefs and put them to the test.

AS YOU WRITE, you may encounter one or all of these pitfalls. Just know that it is perfectly normal. I've been there, and so have all of my previous and current authors. We've all gotten over the finish line though, so I have absolutely no doubt that you can or will too.

That being said, I recognize these are not all of the things you may encounter. Really, I've only scratched the surface, and sometimes authors face blocks that have deeper roots than habit and self-doubt. You may be one of those individuals who needs accountability or someone to bounce ideas off of in order to make it make sense. If this is you or you think you might need more help than what is here, I want to let you know that I'm here for you in that regard. I've included a link on the Thank You page to my contact page so you can reach out to me with any questions about how to personalize this strategy for your specific needs.

Becoming an author is hard work. If there is anything you take away from this, just know that you are not alone and you don't have to do everything yourself. As a writer, you are a part of an elite community. Be proud of that and keep writing.

14

CONCLUSION

"Why do you write?"—four words that have formed both my favorite and least favorite question simultaneously. On one hand, it seems such a silly question, like "Why do birds fly and fish swim?" or "Why do monkeys swing from trees?" These are the sorts of questions that we ask when we are young, to which our parents banally reply, "That's just the way they were made. It's in their nature, so they do it."

I want to say that I write because it's in my nature. I was made to do it. It's no different from a dancer being born to dance or a painter being born to paint. They do it because it's in their nature, and there is something intrinsic in their genetic composition that made them that way. Only, if this were purely nature, why aren't we all writers, dancers, and painters? Perhaps for the same reason that we aren't all flying, swimming, or swinging from trees: we aren't animals.

We're people and, as such, we have something unique within us that gives us an appreciation for art. I'm not talking about the feeling of gratitude or admiration—no, I mean the ability to recognize the value and enjoy the good qualities of something. We humans possess gifts of cognition, of recollection, reasoning, evaluating, and determining. We can impart meaning onto things, and very often we do.

A dancer dances because it is fun to him and he sees it as a way to express himself. The painter paints because she appreciates the fleeting quality of every moment and likes to capture the little changes as if they weren't happening, but static. So, why do writers write? In my opinion, author James Baldwin said it best:

"You write in order to change the world, knowing perfectly well that you probably can't, but also knowing that literature is indispensable to the world... The world changes according to the way people see it, and if you alter, even by a millimeter, the way... people look at reality, then you can change it."

We write because we are stubborn enough to believe that we can change the world one idea at a time. Yet it is that belief that makes such change possible.

You picked up this book because, somewhere inside, you believe that your words can make such a difference, and you've gotten tired of letting time and doubt be the reasons you aren't living up to that potential. Now that you've read this book, you don't have to stay stuck at that same wall. You can take what you've learned and apply it right now. Or tomorrow. Or maybe the day after that... or perhaps someday...

You could absolutely take what you've read, put it on the shelf, and decide that you will get back to it once you have more clarity. I won't judge you, and neither will anyone else. No one ever said that because you've read my book you have to start taking action right away. You have the choice and the right to remain exactly where you are right now, if that's what you want. Just like there is no one out there telling us what to prioritize for the day, there is no force out in the cosmos that will decide your destiny for you.

That's a big, lofty word, "destiny." It comes with so much baggage—thoughts about fate, purpose, and perhaps even eternity. We can make it smaller, though, and say that your destiny is where you will inevitably be in the next one minute. You can decide where you go or where you stay one minute from now and the minute after that and so on. No one here will judge you.

If it sounds like I'm poking, it's because I *am*. I took the time to write you a 45,000-word love letter to help you take action toward your goal. *Of course* I want to see you reach it! I won't judge you, but my wish for you is that you make the choice to use what is in this book today, immediately after you read the final words. Don't let another minute slip by without doing what you know you can.

Why am I so passionate about this? Because if you've made it this far, then I know there is some part of you that is truly ready, that is waiting to burst forth from behind your cage of ribs and spread its wings for the first time. There is an author in you, and they have been waiting for their quill. That author is tired of waiting. Their readers are tired of waiting.

Back in 2019, while I was on a flight to Washington DC to attend training for my new job as a developmental editor with a small publishing company, I listened to a book by Paulo Coelho called *By the River Piedra I Sat Down and Wept*. It was an interesting mix of spirituality, philosophy, and strained romance. I was listening to it because another book by Coelho (*The Alchemist*) had been the catalyst for change that had gotten me on the plane in the first place, and I was ready for more.

There was one scene in that book that stood out to me above the rest. In this scene, the main character, Pilar, is out having wine with her love interest. They are sitting outside on the restaurant patio, and no one is there but the two of them and the wait staff inside. She is hoping, practically begging him, in her head, to make a move and take a risk with her, to take a chance on love because she is already falling for him.

After some time, she takes her glass and sets it at the very edge of the table, to which he says, "It's going to fall."

"Exactly," she replies. She goes on to explain how it's not that big of a deal, and we only make it so because we've been conditioned not to do it. She challenges his worldview, and then urges him repeatedly to "Break the glass."[1]

By repeating this phrase, she was prompting him to break his own mental barriers and limiting beliefs. She needed him to let go because she was already waiting for him to be the person his heart wanted him to be, unrestricted by conditioning and social expectations.

You are like Pilar's beloved, nervous, uncertain, betrayed by your own mind. Pilar is like the world, waiting for you to step out on faith and make your presence known. As I said in chapter 1, your time is now. The moment is happening now.

As I explained in chapter 8, I like to end these types of books with a recap of some of the main ideas. Before I go any further into my wish for you, I want to take a moment to do that with you so you aren't drifting aimlessly in a sea of uncontextualized information (eating a sandwich without the top slice of bread). Here are the core takeaways. If you remember these points, you can write a book easily:

1. One of the biggest reasons aspiring authors don't finish is that they don't have a plan for success. In order to write a book that matters, you have to give yourself a path.
2. Books have been an integral part of human history and advancement of knowledge. They still have a place of relevance and prestige within society.
3. Before you start the journey that is authorship, take time to decide what the goal and purpose of the book are. What would it be worth to you and to your readers for you to actually finish?

4. If you really want to write your book, you have to commit to it. Commit to it so much that you open and dedicate space for it in your calendar. There is time; you just have to decide.
5. Your ideal reader determines all of the important things about your book. They are the key to your topic, your content, and your marketing language. Take time to get to know them as well as you know yourself.
6. Remember that your book's topic is not the same as your subject matter. Your topic is always going to be about helping your reader overcome their specific problem and moving them toward their heart's desire (more accurately, your result for them).
7. Your book should follow a simple three-part structure (beginning, middle, and end), and I termed them "Intro," "Body," "Conclusion." Start with understanding the goal of the book and the specific function of each part. Then choose your book's skeleton.
8. Your Body content is made up of six to twelve steps or pillars your reader needs in order to get from their problem to the result. The best way to arrange these steps is from the most basic or foundational to the more complex or challenging.
9. When you fail to plan, you plan to fail. Reaffirm your writing schedule, set a deadline, and pay close attention to your writing space. Discover your flow state and get ready to show up like never before.
10. Write. Write. *Write!* Don't worry about who's watching (nobody). Don't worry about if it's good. (It will change.) Just make sure it's honest, open, caring, and focused. Feel the fear and do it anyway. Tell stories, don't just teach.

11. Editing is a comprehensive process. I would hire an editor who can take you through at least three of the four mentioned levels of edits. You'll save time and headache and get a better product than if you try to do it yourself.
12. All of your marketing should come from your book topic. That language is optimized to attract your ideal client through your cover art, title, and book description. Whenever you talk about your book, it should always be in terms of how it overcomes the pain point and offers the dream.
13. Writer's block is a myth. You may feel stuck, but you are not blocked. There are blocks that come up, but it's not really a creativity block so much as a breakdown in your process. Sometimes the breakdown is in the execution, sometimes it's in the mind. Find it and get back to writing.

As you leave this book to go do your best work, I want to send you off with a few final thoughts. First and foremost, writing your own book is still a major accomplishment, and the decision to undertake that mission is one that most leave to dreams and wishes. They do this because they believe they have to qualify themselves. The truth is you don't need to have a degree in writing, rhetoric, or journalism to write a book that makes an impact. You are already making an impact; you've "earned" the right to write.

Secondly, even with all of the strategies and systems at play, producing a finished book is a lot of work. There are many nuances that I simply didn't have the space to cover in this book. As I watched the word count creep higher, page by page, I knew there would have to be a stopping point for each idea. When you sit down to write, know that you will feel tired, confused, and even a little lost at points, but that's okay. When you do something new, the expectation is not that you get it right, but that you get it done.

That said, I don't want to tell you that my method is the only way to get it done because you and I both know that's not true. Nor is this book a complete guide to advanced writing technique. There are as many techniques and strategies as there are writers and coaches to use them, and that's okay. This is just one small stop along your journey as a change-maker.

What I will say is that the information and strategies I've outlined are what allowed me to write this book in under thirty days. They are the same as what allowed me to write my first book in just one week and publish three months later, and the process is the very process I've used to help many authors (eight since this January) to finish their manuscripts in record time.

I'm not saying that to sell you on "my" process. It's not really mine. As I said at the beginning of the book, this process is secretly elementary, just adapted to a more sophisticated purpose. What I *am* saying is that I trust this process, and I use it. If I didn't stand behind it, I wouldn't have taken the time to put it in a book as a method to reach your goal. Full stop.

It is my hope—no, I have full confidence that if you take the stories and strategies from this book to heart, do the activities, and take committed action, you will finish your book. It doesn't matter if it takes you seven, thirty, ninety, or 120 days. All that matters is that you create a plan that you can execute to and then do the steps, big and small. It's said that bestselling author Toni Morrison wrote her first novel, *The Bluest Eye*, in fifteen-minute increments each day over five years.

While it's safe to assume your goal is not to take five years, I think Morrison's story is a perfect example of what is possible when we stop asking "if" and start asking "how"—and then implementing once we have an answer. It is the marriage of determination with strategy and faith with action. So I'll close with this. You started your business because you wanted to create transformation. Same as me. As an ~~aspiring~~ transformational author, you are brimming with this potential. With a series of keystrokes, or the swish of a pen, you can literally rewrite your story.

It's time to take up your quill. The world has waited long enough. It's time to write your way to a new life for you and your readers.

The Magician *is card number 1 in Tarot. The character generally associates with skillful communicators. The card symbolizes one's ability to translate ideas into action.*

ACKNOWLEDGMENTS

While I would love to show gratitude to everyone who has supported, encouraged, or inspired me throughout life—because, truly, this book was a lifetime in the making—there are just so many people in that category! If you're not listed here, know that I haven't forgotten you. For the sake of brevity, I'd like to extend thanks to a handful people who have contributed to this book directly or indirectly.

First and foremost, I want to send a shout-out to my cover designer, Emily, of Emily's World of Design. Not only have you produced great work for this cover, but you have taken care of all of my authors. It's an honor to find someone with so much talent, but a blessing to find someone with as much character as you've displayed. Thank you for being on this journey with me now.

To my friends Cory and Yna, thank you. Though you may not know it, your friendship, support, and invaluable knowledge have helped me to become the confident writer and editor I am today. I've learned from both of you and wish to see you both prosper.

I'd like to thank my mentor, Sabah, and my coaches and peers in the Brands That Sell community. I never imagined I would learn so much in such a short timeframe or gain the confidence to create and publish this book in the way that I have. Thank you for the support, the encouragement, and the perfect container to take me to the next level in my business.

Also, it would be remiss of me to leave out my coaches Aaron and Des at the Expert Funnel Incubator. You were the first to help me when I decided to undertake this venture. I wouldn't have made it this far without the foundations you both gave me. Thank you.

To all of my Illuminated Authors—past, present, and future—I say thank you. Thank you for trusting me with your book dreams. Thank you for trusting yourselves with your calling. Without you, there would be no business and no place for this book! (Ha!) More than that, it is through our work together that we grow into the best versions of ourselves.

Last, and certainly not least, I want to acknowledge my family—my mom, dad, and sisters, especially. Each of you has been a pillar in my life that cannot be replaced or undervalued. I could fill another book with the stories and lessons we've learned together, but for now, please accept these few words. No matter what happens, we are family, and that means something. I love you.

Thank you all!

THANK YOU

Thank you for reading my book on book-writing. (Pretty meta, right?) It's been a pleasure to share this passion with you, and I hope that you found true value in my words. Whether you take this work and go on to write many of your own or you choose to stop after your first, know that I am always rooting for you.

To that end, I'd like to offer you **free access** to exclusive bonus content. Using the link below, you'll find training documents, video lessons, and book-planning worksheets taken directly from my program to help you plan your new book.

Free Bonuses:

You should be able to use them to get through the core of this book. Still, I find that some authors struggle to put it all into practice. If you would like my help implementing anything you learned in this book, I invite you to book a free, no-obligation breakthrough session with me.

Free Breakthrough Call:

Finally I'd love to invite you to join my free Facebook community, Illuminated Authors: Write a Book that Makes an Impact and Changes Lives. I share tips, trainings, and resources to support aspiring authors in their mission to make a bigger difference with their books. It's the easiest way to stay up-to-date on free giveaways and new offers, as well as connect with me, directly.

Free Facebook Community:

Good luck on your path to authorship. I look forward to seeing you on the other side, when you're done and published.

ABOUT THE AUTHOR

Andrae D. Smith, Jr. is an editor turned book coach and author of the bestselling book *Facing Racism: The Guide to Overcoming Unconscious Bias and Hidden Prejudice to Be a Part of the Change*. He entered the literary world professionally as a freelance writer and editor in 2014, after studying creative writing and technical editing at Arizona State University. Since then he has served as a beta reader, writing mentor, author trainer, and book editor.

Spurred on by his love of words and stories, Andrae devoted most of his youth to mastering the craft. Writing, to him, was as vital as breathing. Emulating fiction authors like Neil Gaiman, C.S. Lewis, and J.K. Rowling, he tried to replicate their skill at dispelling disbelief and using elaborate lies to communicate significant truth. That was the pinnacle of great writing to which he aspired, and if he could write at that level, he could be someone of consequence and maybe add another much-needed Black voice to the literary world.

So he wrote daily, story after story and page after page of what became his first "bad" novel (a rite of passage for young writers). Once at ASU, he greedily took any creative writing or editing courses he could and bought a small library of books on fiction style and techniques. He joined an online writing forum where he eventually became a mentor and later a volunteer staff reviewer in their writing workshop. Still, he never published anything of his own.

In 2019, after five years in a grueling retail career that arguably almost killed him (a period he sometimes calls the dark ages due to the depressing lack of books and creative expression), Andrae returned to the world of freelance writing and editing full time. Before long, a small publishing company hired him as a developmental editor and introduced him to the power of creative nonfiction—specifically self-help and personal development. This was a deviation from fiction writing, but also a welcome change.

The real value, though, came from working with the clients, real people looking to share their experiences in books that would teach, heal, and guide readers through penetrating personal growth. More often than not, the process of writing was transformative for the authors as well. Perhaps he was living vicariously through them, but he took great personal satisfaction seeing his writers cross the threshold into inspirational authorship.

After the murder of George Floyd in May of 2020, he combined all of his years of experience with a roused hunger for social justice and decided to write his own book. He published *Facing Racism* on September 8, 2020. While he did get to bask in the surrealism of becoming an author, sending thank-you messages and promising signed copies to readers as far away as Hawaii and Maine, it was the reviews that showed him what he had really accomplished. His readers found themselves inspired, empowered, and deeply moved, and Andrae came to realize just how significant his work as an editor was.

Although fiction writing will always be his first love (one to which he hopes to return someday), Andrae has developed a passion for helping people transform their lives through creative nonfiction, whether they are other authors or the readers they serve. Though he may only write a handful of books in his lifetime, with few becoming bestsellers, as an editor and coach he can reach thousands of people through his clients' work and be a part of something larger than himself.

As a publishing professional, Andrae hopes to create an avenue for writers of various levels and backgrounds to publish where, traditionally, there may be little room. His aim is to connect writers with a message to the audiences who need them most.

APPENDIX 1

PUTTING YOUR BOOK TOGETHER

The main body of this book focused primarily on building your book blueprint and writing your first draft. I understand that there is so much more that goes into a book. I truly wish I had more room to give you all of the knowledge I've amassed, only that would take far more than just 45,000 words. Even so, I wanted to use this small space to tell you a little about how to put your book together once it's all done.

In chapter 8, I told you to think of your book as having three sections. In reality, you can think of it as having five:
- Front matter
- Introduction
- Body
- Conclusion
- Back matter

Front and back matter are like bookends for your main content. They are essential pieces to any professionally published work, so you'll want to make sure you have them before your book goes to print.

There are specific elements you will need in each section in order for your book to look and feel clean and well-organized.

I've listed them here for you, but will leave it up to you to determine whether you need each element.

FRONT MATTER

- Advance Praise (optional) – Short reviews from early readers.

- Half Title Page – Title of book with no subtitle, author, or publisher. This is optional, but standard for printed books.

- Title Page – Title of book with author and publisher.

- Copyright – Declares copyright, ISBN, and publisher information.

- Dedication (optional) – Short blurb dedicating the book to someone.

- Contents – Table of Contents.

- Foreword (optional) – A brief introduction written by someone other than the author. Best if this person is a prominent figure in the industry.

- Preface (optional) – A brief look at the origins of the book.

BACK MATTER

- Acknowledgements – Brief section naming and thanking contributors of the work.

- Thank You – A special page thanking readers, offering gifts, and supplying opportunities to stay in touch with the author.

• About the Author – A one- to two-page bio or narrative about the author.

• Appendix (optional) – Additional information outside of the scope of the main content.

• Notes (optional) – Endnotes listed here.

• Glossary (optional) – List of notable terms and definitions for reference.

• Bibliography (optional) – A formal citation list for all sources and references used in the book.

Including all of these sections is not required. Not every book will need an appendix or glossary. I have restricted this list to what you might expect to see in a client-conversion book like yours. (This is a book that's designed to turn readers into clients.)

If it doesn't say "optional" next to it, assume it is strongly advised.

APPENDIX 2

TURN YOUR COURSE INTO A BOOK

You may have come to this book as someone who has an existing program or course and you just need an outline or framework for turning that into a compact book. You can use the framework below as a guide:

PREFACE
Purpose: After reading this section, the reader should understand who You are, and why you've written this book

Intro:
Identify who this book is for and Define the Problem that exists
Clarify the need for a solution. (Why is a solution needed? What is at stake?)

Body:
Introduce yourself – What's her background and experience with this problem?
Why do you care about this problem?
Why/how did you develop your solution?

Conclusion:
What do you hope to achieve in this book?

INTRODUCTION

Purpose: After reading this section, the reader should understand the purpose and scope of this book, what it is and is not, and how to approach the material within.

Intro:
 Affirm the topic of the book, the problem, and your proposed solution.

Body:
  What is this book?
  What is it not?
  What is in the book?
  How should read the material?

Conclusion:
  What Does you hope to achieve in this book?
  What can the reader expect from this book?
  What attitudes/beliefs should they maintain (or release) to get the most out of it?

MODULE 1:

Clear Purpose Statement: After reading this chapter, the prospect/reader/client will be able to be/do/have….
Intro: Set up / story
Body: Training Case Studies + Training
Conclusion: Final Thoughts + Action/Exercise

MODULE 2:

Clear Purpose Statement: After reading this chapter, the prospect/reader/client will be able to be/do/have….
Intro: Set up / story
Body: Training Case Studies + Training
Conclusion: Final Thoughts + Action/Exercise

MODULE 3:
Clear Purpose Statement: *After reading this chapter, the prospect/reader/client will be able to be/do/have….*
Intro: Set up / story
Body: Training Case Studies + Training
Conclusion: Final Thoughts + Action/Exercise

MODULE 4:
Clear Purpose Statement: *After reading this chapter, the prospect/reader/client will be able to be/do/have….*
Intro: Set up / story
Body: Training Case Studies + Training
Conclusion: Final Thoughts + Action/Exercise

MODULE 5:
Clear Purpose Statement: *After reading this chapter, the prospect/reader/client will be able to be/do/have….*
Intro: Set up / story
Body: Training Case Studies + Training
Conclusion: Final Thoughts + Action/Exercise

MODULE 6:
Clear Purpose Statement: *After reading this chapter, the prospect/reader/client will be able to be/do/have….*
Intro: Set up / story
Body: Training Case Studies + Training
Conclusion: Final Thoughts + Action/Exercise

MODULE 7:
Clear Purpose Statement: *After reading this chapter, the prospect/reader/client will be able to be/do/have….*
Intro: Set up / story
Body: Training Case Studies + Training
Conclusion: Final Thoughts + Action/Exercise

CONCLUSION

Purpose: After reading this chapter, the reader should understand this book's essential message, their role in the desired change, and any final tips on how to implement this.

Intro:

Acknowledge the reader's commitment in reaching the end

Tie up loose ends, close out open stories

Body:

Recap the journey

Emphasize the book's core tenets/messages (What should the reader's know and be able to do?)

Any last tips?

Conclusion:

Share Your vision for the future and hopes for her reader.

Where to go from here?

THANK YOU

Purpose: The reader will learn how to receive additional support as well as receive a gift or lead magnet.

NOTES

3. THE ILLUMINATION METHOD

1. S.M.A.R.T. is a common goal-setting acronym that can vary slightly. In this case, it stands for Specific, Measurable, Attainable, Relevant, and Time-bound.

4. WHY A BOOK?

1. *Harry Potter and the Order of the Phoenix* is the fifth book in J.K. Rowling's famed *Harry Potter* franchise.
2. Thakur, Tara & Mahesh, Chanda. (2016). Enhancement in Shooting ability of Basketball players through Meditation. *ISCA Journal of Physical Education SCIENCES*. 4. 2320-9011.

6. IDENTIFY AND DEFINE YOUR READER

1. OED Online. June 2021. Oxford University Press. http://www.oed.com/viewdictionaryentry/Entry/11125 (accessed August 19, 2021).

11. EDITING SECRETS

1. As special note, the term Substantive Editing is sometimes used interchangeably with line editing or developmental editing depending on whom you are speaking with. In some cases, it is considered an umbrella term for both services together. Be sure to ask your editor what they mean by it.

14. CONCLUSION

1. Coelho, Paulo. "Break the Glass!" Paulo Coelho, February 23, 2013. https://paulocoelhoblog.com/2013/03/15/break-the-glass.

www.ingramcontent.com/pod-product-compliance
Lightning Source LLC
Chambersburg PA
CBHW051431290426
44109CB00016B/1509